THE CONSCIOUS PARENT'S GUIDE TO

Asperger's Syndrome

A mindful approach for helping
your child succeed

William Stillman

Adamsmedia
Avon, Massachusetts

DEDICATION

For mindful parents everywhere.

Published by
Adams Media, a division of F+W Media, Inc.
57 Littlefield Street, Avon, MA 02322. U.S.A.
www.adamsmedia.com

Contains material adapted from *The Everything® Parent's Guide to Children with Asperger's Syndrome, 2nd Edition* by William Stillman, copyright © 2010, 2005 by F+W Media, Inc., ISBN 10: 1-4405-0394-X, ISBN 13: 978-1-4405-0394-8.

ISBN 10: 1-4405-9314-0
ISBN 13: 978-1-4405-9314-7
eISBN 10: 1-4405-9315-9
eISBN 13: 978-1-4405-9315-4

Printed in the United States of America.

10   9   8   7   6   5   4   3   2   1

Library of Congress Cataloging-in-Publication Data

Stillman, William.
The conscious parent's guide to Asperger's syndrome / William Stillman.
   pages cm
Includes index.
 ISBN 978-1-4405-9314-7 (pb) -- ISBN 1-4405-9314-0 (pb) -- ISBN 978-1-4405-9315-4 (ebook)
-- ISBN 1-4405-9315-9 (ebook)
1. Asperger's syndrome--Popular works. 2. Parent and child--Popular works. I. Title.
RC553.A88S837 2015
618.92'858832--dc23
                    2015030436

Cover design by Frank Rivera.

This book is available at quantity discounts for bulk purchases.
For information, please call 1-800-289-0963.

Introduction

Long ago and far away, kids who drew detailed diagrams of spacecraft, created intricate models of the human digestive system, spent all their free time reading about medieval cathedrals, or enjoyed reciting complex dinosaur names—and preferred those isolated activities over playtime with peers—were labeled. The labels were a reflection of a so-called socially inappropriate desire to be absorbed with things, instead of people. Words often used to describe such kids may have included *gifted, moody, antisocial, irritable, obsessed, geek, brainiac,* or even *stoic.* They may have been thought of as outsiders, with no or few friends. As adults, they may have been considered odd and eccentric, loners or hermits.

Fortunately, today we are shifting our perception of what we now know to be Asperger's Syndrome. We are learning more about Asperger's as a milder "cousin" on the autism spectrum. (Some equate Asperger's with "high-functioning autism.") We are accepting Asperger's as a legitimate framework to describe a unique experience. Slowly but surely, we are moving beyond stereotypes in our collective understanding of children with Asperger's. We are recognizing their different ways of thinking, different ways of perceiving the world, and different ways of being. As we grow in our sensitivity and understanding, we are better able to support and celebrate the child with Asperger's Syndrome. Instead of labeling a child as "obsessed," we may now praise her giftedness and balance her needs to find a social niche.

We are learning more and more about autism all the time, but we're only just beginning to scratch the surface of Asperger's Syndrome. Asperger's is still a very new consideration for parents and many prescribing doctors. There is much to explore on this broad learning curve: social differences, mental health, sensory sensitivities, and coping strategies that will be of lifelong value. Parents may become overwhelmed with clinical information that reinforces their child's perceived deficits—the things she is not expected to be able to do in life. Other areas that may prompt confusion include options regarding learning and educational placement, training and programming, and therapies and techniques. Well-intentioned neighbors and family members may offer their perspectives based on what they've heard or read, whether it has any factual basis or not. Considerations for a child's future living arrangements, adult relationships, and viable vocations may create family and marital stress.

Throughout this journey, it will be important for parents to remain grounded in one thought: We are all more alike than different. Understanding the child with Asperger's Syndrome is a learning opportunity for parents, siblings, and extended family.

When we foster an appreciation of the unique ways we *all* participate in the world, we are poised to better value those with Asperger's. When we actively project new and positive ways of supporting the child with Asperger's, she will respond in equally positive ways. The result is that a mutual relationship is strengthened tenfold, and a ripple effect occurs.

The Conscious Parent's Guide to Asperger's Syndrome aids parents in making balanced, informed choices about their child and her future. Ideally, this journey is a partnership between parent and child in decision-making and education about Asperger's Syndrome. More than ever, a path of opportunity lies before parents of children with Asperger's Syndrome.

Contents

 **CHAPTER 1**

Conscious Parenting

Being a conscious parent is all about building strong, sustainable bonds with your children through mindful living and awareness. Traditional power-based parenting techniques that promote compliance and obedience can disconnect you from your children. Conscious parenting, on the other hand, helps you develop a positive emotional connection with your child. Through empathetic understanding and tolerance you create a safe environment where your children feel their concerns are truly being heard. When you find yourself in a stressful situation with your child, rather than reacting with anger or sarcasm, conscious parenting reminds you to instead take a step back, reflect, and look for a peaceful solution. This approach benefits all children, especially those with Asperger's Syndrome. When your child is diagnosed with Asperger's, it can seem like all you're hearing are the negatives—your child's "disabilities" rather than his abilities. But the conscious parent knows how to temper this information to create a balanced perspective. Your child with Asperger's has much to offer in the form of gifts and talents. Adopting the conscious parenting philosophy can relieve your stress and improve your child's self-image.

The Benefits of Conscious Parenting

It is important to note that conscious parenting is not a set of rules or regulations that you must follow, but rather it is a system of beliefs. Conscious parents engage and connect with their children, using mindful and positive discipline rather than punishment. They try to be present when they're spending time with their children, avoiding distractions such as TV and social media. Conscious parents respect their children and accept them as they are. The most important part of conscious parenting is building an emotional connection with your child so you can understand the underlying reasons for behavior.

> Conscious parenting is about listening with full attention, and embracing a nonjudgmental acceptance of yourself and your child. As you engage in the act of *becoming*, you will discover a heightened sense of emotional awareness of yourself and your child, a clearer self-regulation in the parenting relationship, and a greater compassion for yourself and your child.

Conscious parenting brings with it a number of benefits including improved communication, stronger relationships, and the feeling of greater happiness and satisfaction in life. Some of these benefits appear immediately, while others take some time to emerge. The benefits of conscious parenting and mindfulness are a result of making these habits a part of your daily life. With practice, conscious parenting becomes an integral part of who and how you are in the world, and will in turn become a central part of who your child is as well.

AWARENESS

One of the first benefits of conscious parenting that you (and your child) will see is a heightened awareness of yourself and your inner life, including your emotions, thoughts, and feelings. As you become more aware of these various forces moving within you, you can begin to watch them rise without being at their mercy. For example, when you are aware that you are becoming angry, you have a choice about whether to act from that anger or attend to that feeling directly.

Mindfulness is the practice of being attentive in every moment, and noticing what is taking place both inside and outside of you without making a value judgment. It is the practice of purposefully seeing your thoughts, emotions, experiences, and surroundings as they arise. Simply put, mindfulness is the act of paying attention.

As you become more skilled at noticing the thoughts and feelings that arise, you will begin to notice them more quickly, maybe even before they start to affect your actions. This awareness is itself a powerful tool. It opens up the possibility of saying, "Hey, I'm pretty mad right now . . ." as opposed to yelling at somebody you care about because you were upset about something else. It can do exactly the same thing for your child, helping him to learn to communicate about his feelings rather than just react from that place of emotion. As with most things, children will learn this best by seeing it modeled by the adults in their lives.

WELL-BEING

Conscious parents understand that all they do and say over the course of each day *matters*. It is a sense of the *now*, being present in the moment without regard or worry for the past or future. When you become more mindful, you may find that you become more accepting of the things in life that you can't change and experience less stress. The net result is greater satisfaction and enjoyment of whatever each day has to offer. This sense of well-being offers a satisfaction and contentment in knowing that we are who we are intended to be, doing precisely what we are designed for at the moment.

As human beings, we each possess the tools for contributing something of value. Assess your gifts and talents—those personality traits and skills that make you unique—and determine how to employ them to enhance your parenting. If you take a full accounting of yourself—good, bad, and indifferent—and *own* the sum total of your individual experience, you are taking the first step toward conscious parenting.

EMPATHY

The awareness you gain has the practical purpose of redefining your perception of yourself and your compassionate understanding of your child. For example, like someone diagnosed with Asperger's Syndrome, you may engage in actions or activities that work for you but may be perceived as eccentric, odd, or peculiar by others. You may have a specific sequence mapped out for the manner in which you grocery shop, run errands, or tend to the yard work. It makes no sense to anyone else but is perfectly logical to you. You may have a particular way of organizing things on your desk at work. You may even become distressed or infuriated if anyone "messes" with your system. Your workspace may appear disheveled, but you can lay your hands on the exact data report in question upon request.

Another example is the way you type at a keyboard. You may be a speed typist, hitting the keys without looking at them. Or you may be someone who was never able to "hard-wire" your brain to type with both hands simultaneously. To compensate, you may use one finger on each hand to hunt and peck your way to successful typing. Perhaps you can use only one finger on one hand to type. In the end, isn't the result of the facile typist and the hunt-and-peck typist the same? Does it, then, make any difference how either arrived at the same result?

Remember these examples as you learn to appreciate your child's unique way of being in the world. This will provide you with the patience to allow your child's unique thought processes to unfold.

Giving Your Child Full Attention

The child with Asperger's is often inherently gentle and exquisitely sensitive. It is imperative that negative thoughts and feelings not be projected upon the child or communicated directly in front of him. When this negativity transpires consistently enough, a self-fulfilling prophecy occurs. That is, if you hear people refer to you only in disparaging, disrespectful terms, you believe it and, eventually, you become it. You reflect back what people project upon you because you believe it is what they expect. After all, it's how you've been defined all along. Being so sensitive, the child with Asperger's may naturally internalize, replay, and agonize over all of this to no end. So you see how easily a vicious cycle can result and even repeat itself over a lifetime.

Instead of feeling worn out by your child's intense interests, take a moment to indulge him and listen carefully. Or when you catch your child doing something that displays his amazing gifts, praise him lavishly. Your outpouring of attention and genuine interest will come back to you tenfold.

However, conscious parenting can be a powerful antidote that counteracts the negative projections and perceptions you or your child might experience. As a conscious parent, you can create a positive, nonjudgmental, and loving environment that your child can count on. With the emotional connections that you form with your child, you celebrate your child as an individual, with a unique personality. You let your child know that you understand his behavior as the way he perceives the world.

Negative thoughts and feelings should be shed in favor of positive perspectives. Your child is a child, first and foremost. A beautiful, entirely unique, magnificently gorgeous human being with as many faults and frailties as gifts and talents; the same is true of everyone. In childhood, your child will rely upon you and his family to provide a solid foundation of self-esteem. Equipped with a strong sense of self-worth, he will be better prepared to enter into a life that will likely present many challenges. Much of your time and energy will be expended in raising, counseling, and disciplining your child in ways that he will understand. It is important to try to equalize those occasions by reinforcing your love and appreciation of his gifts and talents.

It is speculated that some of the world's greatest thinkers, innovators, and artists have had Asperger's Syndrome. They form a long list of famous personalities: Ludwig van Beethoven, Isaac Newton, Albert Einstein, Thomas Jefferson, Thomas Edison, Vincent van Gogh, Emily Dickinson, Henry Ford, Mark Twain, Alfred Hitchcock, H.P. Lovecraft, Andy Warhol, Charles Schulz, Bill Gates, and Michael Jackson. In a historical perspective, your child with Asperger's Syndrome is in outstanding company.

At every opportunity, remind your child how special he is to you. Tell him that you are delighted when he shares his astronomy charts with you. Laugh at his impressions of cartoon characters and tell him what a terrific actor he is. Highlight your child's gifts when talking with family and friends. Prominently display his works of art. You may be amazed at the long-lasting impact these moments will have as they buoy your child into adolescence and young adulthood.

Understanding Behavior

Clinical psychologist Herbert Lovett, PhD, an advocate for people with special needs, wrote that we should think of two ideas when dealing with difficult behavior: first, "People have good reasons for doing what they do." And second, "People are doing the very best they know how to with what they've got." As a parent of a child with Asperger's, you'll often be faced with situations that can benefit from stopping and thinking of these two statements.

Here's one example: Upon meeting a severely overweight man while in the company of his parents and others, a preteen boy with Asperger's Syndrome asked the man in a loud, clear voice how it felt to be "fat." The incident caused some people to conceal smirks while others felt embarrassment at the boy's candor. The man in question surely felt some degree of humiliation as well. In addressing the situation, the parent of a typical child might scold the child for his insensitive and rude remark. But how would you respond using Dr. Lovett's philosophy?

1. Did the boy have good reasons for doing what he was doing? What was his motivation in asking the heavyset man such a blunt and blatant question? The boy was himself overweight for his age. In asking the man how it felt to be fat, he was attempting to legitimately learn some important information. He was knowledgeable of the inherent health risks and issues that may be associated with being overweight. He was projecting himself into the future by envisioning himself as an overweight adult, not unlike the man.

2. Was the boy doing the very best he knew how to in the moment? The parent of a typical child might conclude that the child should have known enough to withhold such a crass remark and was deliberately creating an embarrassing scene. However, the boy had never been privately counseled not to make remarks about people's weight in public. Nor had anyone previously told him that the word "fat" was usually highly offensive when used to describe someone.

Does this mean that the child with Asperger's is never deliberately a troublemaker? Of course not; kids are kids. Your challenge is to discern what motivates your child with Asperger's Syndrome and separate that from jumping to conclusions about typical smart-alecky kid behavior.

Conscious Parenting Tips

Conscious parenting is a *process* that is as unique and individual as each family is unique. Parenting in a mindful manner comes with an authentic appreciation for your gifts and talents (and those of your child), as well as an understanding for how best to employ those gifts and talents to help your child grow to be a happy, successful member of society. Think of this style of raising your child as *parenting with grace*.

Having a gracious approach means understanding the following:

O There is safety in sameness and comfort in what is familiar.

O In order to feel safe and comfortable, the child must have control.

Think about the times when your child appeared most content, comfortable, and at ease. Was he enjoying playing a solitary computer game? Was he alone in his bedroom, drawing whales and sharks? Or was he directing the play of his siblings and friends? In these instances, was your child engaged in a favored, pleasurable activity? Was it a repetitive activity from which comfort is derived? And during this activity, did your child have control? The response to these questions is likely yes.

Now, reverse the situations and remove the elements of safety, comfort, and control. Say the computer unexpectedly locks up and the video game is interrupted. A sibling won't turn down his music while your child is attempting to concentrate on the details of his marine life drawings. Or a friend decides she doesn't want to be "bossed" by your child and opts out of their playtime. These situations are unexpected and unpredictable. Your child feels unsafe, uncomfortable, and out of control when the unpredictable occurs and wins out.

Your child may feel overwhelmed by the loss of control. He may act out in a variety of undesirable ways. But if you take a moment to understand what's going on, you'll realize that he has good reasons for his behavior and is doing the best he knows how in order to cope with the loss of safety and comfort. His reaction is a logical progression of that escalation until he learns other coping strategies. When you are present in your parenting, you understand this and you can communicate your understanding to your child. Your emotional attachment to your child means that you can let your child know that you understand *why* he is behaving in a certain way, even as you work together to find a better way of reacting the next time.

Think of the areas in which your child is naturally gifted. Does his comprehension of computer programs exceed that of many adults? Does he enjoy describing the exact alignment of our solar system's planets, identifying each by correct name, placement, and color? Does he assume the personality traits of a favorite cartoon character with uncanny accuracy, down to mimicking lines of dialogue? Or does he have the quiet reverence to render amazing watercolors? These passions are the areas of talent to recognize and encourage as uniquely your child's own.

Your recognition of Asperger's Syndrome as a positive attribute and your appreciation of your child's gifts and talents will make your home and family a place where he is unconditionally loved and understood. Many parents just like you have made this mindful-parenting commitment and can readily attest to the profound, loving impact it has made on their lives.

 **CHAPTER 2**

Defining Asperger's Syndrome

As a conscious parent, you need to know what your child is going through so you can empathize with her feelings and emotions. With that in mind, it is important to understand the history and characteristics of Asperger's Syndrome so you can be ready for any questions or concerns your child may have. She may have a natural curiosity about what this condition is, what a diagnosis of Asperger's means, or even whether she will ever be free of it. These are normal concerns and you will be an immense benefit to your child if you are informed about Asperger's and ready to open a dialogue with her when she comes to you. This chapter will discuss the history and characteristics of Asperger's Syndrome to help you prepare to answer your child's questions.

Background and History

Asperger's Syndrome was first defined in 1944 by Hans Asperger, an Austrian pediatrician who studied social interactions, communication, and behavior in children who had unique ways of acting and interacting. In 1943, he studied a group of children, mostly boys, who had difficulty interacting in socially acceptable ways. The children appeared intrinsic or self-centered—not necessarily selfish, but they preferred to keep to themselves. Most were not physically adept and were rather uncoordinated. The children experienced no cognitive delays and were, in fact, quite articulate, with a strong command of vocabulary. The children engaged in repetitive physical actions, or were fascinated with nuances of timetables or the mechanics of certain objects such as clocks.

Asperger published his findings in 1944 in a paper titled "Autistic Psychopathy in Childhood." By today's standards the title is alarming, but in using the word "psychopathy," Asperger did not intend to describe mentally ill, violent behavior; he was using the clinically acceptable jargon of the day. Asperger's findings were the first documented collection of traits now used to diagnose Asperger's Syndrome.

Hans Asperger's findings were published nearly simultaneously with the research of Leo Kanner, another doctor who, in 1943, first distinguished the traits of autism. Because Asperger's paper was published in German and Kanner's in English, Kanner's research received broader distribution and was subsequently popularized.

Unknown to Asperger, a psychiatrist named Leo Kanner was conducting similar research at Johns Hopkins University at about the same time. In 1943, Kanner chose the word "autism" (from the Greek word *autos*, or "self") to describe a group of children who shared similar personality traits, engaged in solitary actions, and struggled with communicating effectively, reliably, and understandably.

On the Autism Spectrum

Despite the growing recognition of autism as an acceptable diagnosis during the 1950s and 1960s, Hans Asperger's research went largely unnoticed. Still, there were individuals who experienced autistic-like symptoms but did not have the cognitive differences usually found in those with autism. At the time, such individuals were diagnosed with mental illness or nervous anxiety. Some were institutionalized or imprisoned because of their odd behavior or because they were gullible and easily manipulated into making poor or dangerous choices.

A popular theory to explain the alleged distance felt between parents— mothers in particular—and their children with autism was called "refrigerator mother theory," which referred to the supposed aloofness or indifference shown by mothers unable to connect with their children. According to this theory, mothers who were unable or unwilling to connect with their children caused the children to exhibit autistic behaviors. In fact, Asperger's Syndrome is no one's fault.

In 1981, British psychiatrist Lorna Wing revived Hans Asperger's findings in a research paper of her own. This eventually led to the reclassification of autistic experiences in the *Diagnostic and Statistical Manual of Mental Disorders (DSM)*.

Some recent theories being researched to explain the increasing prevalence of autism and Asperger's Syndrome include genetics, environmental factors (pregnant mothers' exposure to or ingestion of chemical elements), or children's immune system reactions to certain childhood vaccinations. There is currently no prenatal or other biological exam to test for Asperger's Syndrome.

Goodbye to Asperger's?

Since 1952, the *DSM* has been published in the United States by the American Psychiatric Association, with revisions appearing periodically. As of this writing, it is in its fifth edition, published in 2013. Most U.S. clinicians and psychiatrists use the *DSM* to measure various mental-emotional symptoms against the criteria in the manual in order to make a diagnosis. With the latest edition, Asperger's Syndrome is no longer a solitary diagnosis of its own but is included in the category of autism spectrum disorder (ASD).

The *Diagnostic and Statistical Manual* catalogs a wide range of mental health and related experiences. It is the foremost reference guide used by psychiatrists, psychologists, social workers, mental health professionals, therapists, counselors, and nurses, to name a few. It provides a framework to diagnose someone's experience according to symptoms.

A BLENDING MIX

Does this mean that Asperger's has "gone away" in terms of its clinical distinction in the *DSM*? First, just because Asperger's is described as on the autism spectrum doesn't mean there's no such thing as Asperger's. It is still a legitimate experience and an authentic way of being, thinking, and comprehending the world. Second, even though the experience of Asperger's Syndrome isn't named as a specific diagnosis in the 2013 *DSM-5*, many medical professionals still use the term "Asperger's Syndrome" to describe this particular segment of the autism spectrum.

SELF-ADVOCATE PERSPECTIVE

What does the *DSM* alteration mean for people with Asperger's and how might the change affect their ability to continue advocating for themselves? Michael John Carley, executive director of GRASP (Global and Regional Asperger Syndrome Partnership) and the author of *Asperger's from the Inside Out*, weighs the pros and cons of the issue:

> The cons will all occur in the short term. Not only will many of our members struggle with a terminology that has regrettably carried with it different associations, but the social service world carries definite possibilities of chaos after the change is implemented. How many service agencies will deny benefits to our folks because the

agency uses the old terminology, whilst the applicant uses the new? How many school districts will deny an appropriate education because they use the new terminology, whilst the family in need doesn't have the money to get a new evaluation that adheres to the *DSM-5*? How much money will have to be spent by disproportionately poorer folks to get that new evaluation? And how bad will the inevitable resentment be toward those providing diagnostic services, as they reap untold amounts of dough from the world's need to adapt to this new book? *Lots* of internal as well as external disarray.

The pros, however, are for the long term. GRASP has always advocated that the spectrum's complexity went against our very human need to compartmentalize. After all, it is really hard for the average Joe on the street to swallow the idea that people like Albert Einstein, Thomas Jefferson, and Emily Dickinson could possibly have different variations of the same condition as someone who might never speak (as in some with autism). But the fact is that every clinical attempt to draw a line in the sand where autism becomes Asperger's and vice versa has proved false in practice, mostly because in varying proportion, everyone learns and adapts as life goes on. It simply is that complicated. The stigma of the words "Asperger's Syndrome" still has a long way to go, but the stigma of the word "autism" is unfortunately, still very dark. This change may push us (or force us) *all* toward digesting how complex this condition really is, so that we stop looking for a "picture" of autism or Asperger's that reflects what we see in the mirror.

Many of GRASP's members diagnosed with Asperger's Syndrome refer to themselves as "autistic" or "having autism." Others don't. I, personally, have always used Asperger's Syndrome to describe myself because that's what my two diagnoses called it (and I'm very careful not to assume that I'm a doctor). I also try to be cognizant of others' resentment, whether I find their reasoning worthy of my respect or not. But that doesn't mean that I don't cognitively agree with those diagnosed with Asperger's Syndrome who call themselves autistic. It's just that being right is not always what's important.

As of this writing, it remains to be seen how the changes will or won't affect Asperger's Syndrome in terms of diagnosing, treating, supporting, and appreciating the condition. But knowledge is power; please equip yourself and your child with as many strategies, tips, tricks, and coping tactics as possible (many of which are in this very book) in order to persevere come what may.

Asperger's Defined

The 1994 *DSM-IV* was the first edition of the *DSM* to formally recognize Asperger's Syndrome, which was categorized under the general heading of pervasive developmental disorders (PDD). There were several other diagnoses that fell under the PDD heading. These were:

O Autistic disorder (known as autism)

O Rett disorder (or Rett Syndrome)

O Childhood disintegrative disorder

O Asperger's disorder (known as Asperger's Syndrome)

O Pervasive developmental disorder not otherwise specified (or PDD-NOS)

These were all subcategories of the PDD diagnosis, collectively grouped under the PDD heading because of the similarities of symptoms related to challenges in communication, social interaction, and so-called stereotyped behaviors, interests, and activities. Autism is the most prevalent of these experiences, more common than Down Syndrome or childhood cancer.

Some clinicians consider the term "high-functioning autism" (HFA) synonymous with Asperger's Syndrome, but the generally accepted distinction is the presence of a speech delay in the former experience, which is absent in classic Asperger's. The *DSM* does not presently define HFA, so it may or may not apply to a child with Asperger's.

Asperger's Syndrome has been diagnosed in children as young as three. Little is known about Asperger's at present. There is no single known cause, although there are many theories. It is a neurological condition that primarily creates challenges in understanding social interactions. Asperger's is not a disease or chronic mental illness. It is a natural, life-long experience.

CLINICAL CRITERIA

As of 2013, symptoms that were previously considered indicators of Asperger's Syndrome are now included under the diagnostic umbrella heading of autism spectrum disorder (ASD). As currently defined by the *DSM-5*, a child with ASD may have the following traits:

O Persistent difficulties in social communication and interaction, such as social and emotional "sharing" or failing to initiate or respond to interactions

O Challenges with eye contact and interpretation of facial expressions and body language

O Difficulty maintaining peer relationships

O Repeating certain behaviors, and having very specific interests or activities, such as repeating a body motion or sound, or lining up objects

O Insisting on the sameness of routines

O Very strong, unusual interests

O Over- or underreaction to pain, temperature, sounds, textures, or smelling or touching things

O Fascination with light or movement

To be considered indicators of ASD, these symptoms should be present:

O Are apparent in an individual's early stages of development (although they may not fully manifest until later in life)

O Cause significant impairment in the individual's quality of life and ability to function

O Aren't better explained by another clinical diagnosis or delay

A more thorough and complete accounting of the newly revised clinical criteria for ASD may be found online at *www.autismspeaks.org*. The *DSM-5* indicates that individuals previously diagnosed with Asperger's Syndrome under the old *DSM-IV* should now be considered to have ASD. Those same individuals may, of course, continue to identify themselves as having Asperger's if they so choose.

The word "disorder" may not seem like a good way to describe your child's personal experience, but it is the way that clinicians currently refer to Asperger's Syndrome. Outside of a doctor's office, you may wish to use the word "difference" or the phrase "different way of being" when you feel the need to describe your child's experience, if at all. Your child's physician, educators, or school psychologist may be able to recommend literature in addition to the *DSM*.

Characteristics of Asperger's Syndrome and ASD

One of the new distinctions introduced in the *DSM-5* is the inclusion of sensory sensitivities in the description of ASD. Examples might be that of the child who screams and covers her ears when a nearby ambulance sounds its siren. Or the child who can't tolerate the feel of Jell-O or pudding in her mouth. These seeming "overreactions" are sensory sensitivities, a commonality shared with people with so-called "classic" autism.

Your child may be described as "exquisitely sensitive." Because of this, her entire nervous system—her senses and emotions—may be routinely affected by stimulation others filter out naturally. Many children with ASD exhibit this hypersensitivity.

HEARING SENSITIVITY

A child with hypersensitive hearing may cry and recoil from a variety of sounds. She reacts in this way because in a very real sense, she is physically hurting from the intensity of the noise. The most offensive sounds are those that are not only very loud and startling but also unpredictable, meaning there's no telling when or where they will occur with any certainty. The most commonly hurtful sounds for someone with especially sensitive hearing include: dogs barking; babies crying; crowd noises; vacuum cleaners; police, ambulance, and fire engine sirens, or cars backfiring; loud music or television programs; public announcement systems and intercoms; people tapping, clicking, or snapping fingers or objects (such as a pencil); and people laughing, talking, or sneezing loudly.

TASTE AND SMELL SENSITIVITIES

Certain smells (especially food scents and perfumes or toiletries) and tastes may also be overwhelming. On occasion, a child may gag and vomit in reaction to the sensation of the smell or texture of foods. Unable to explain herself in the moment, the child may bolt from the environment if the smells or tastes become too much for her to handle.

VISUAL SENSITIVITY

Because many people with Asperger's are very visual in how they absorb and process information, they may also become easily overwhelmed by too many visual details in a single environment (think Walmart on a Saturday afternoon). The number of moving, flapping, or spinning objects paired with the vivid mix of colors and combined with a large number of people in a single location can push the child with Asperger's into sensory overload.

Light that is too intense can also cause pain and discomfort. Overhead fluorescent lighting is especially troublesome for many people with Asperger's and autism. In addition to its intensity, fluorescent lighting may flicker and buzz. The flickering and buzzing may go completely unnoticed by others but will become unbearable for the child with heightened sensitivities.

TOUCH SENSITIVITY

Finally, the sensation of touch may be equally overwhelming. Being hugged, patted on the head or back, or picked up—especially unpredictably and without warning or permission—may cause the child to cry, bite, or even hit. The problem is that children, particularly small children, often tend to be hugged, patted, and picked up simply because they're adorable.

The texture of certain clothing fabrics worn against the skin may create discomfort and physical irritation as well. This sensation has been likened to one's flesh being rubbed raw with sandpaper. For some, cotton and natural fiber clothes are a must to ward off skin welts and rashes. Conversely, other children with Asperger's may welcome (and seek out) the sensory input provided by the deep-pressured touch. They enjoy strong bear hugs, massage, burrowing under sofa cushions and mattresses, or self-swaddling in comforters and sleeping bags. This is clinically called "hyposensitive" or having an under-sensitive response.

It is important to appreciate that none of these reactions are attention-seeking or deliberately bad behaviors. They are a genuine reaction to extreme disturbances in the child's immediate environment. For example, one mother assumed her son was engaging her in a power struggle when he refused to wear the new blue jeans he had picked out in the store and that she purchased for him. Stopping to have a conversation instead of an argument revealed the true problem—they felt stiff and scratched his skin when he put them on. Washing the new jeans several times to soften them made them physically tolerable, and the conflict was resolved without further incident. Hypersensitivity may seem like overreaction to you sometimes, but take the time to listen and validate your child's feelings. Often, you can both work together to help make your child's day-to-day experiences more comfortable.

COMMUNICATION ISSUES

Children with Asperger's Syndrome or ASD often exhibit "flat affect" expressions and somewhat different speech patterns. A flat affect refers to facial expressions that are fixed or "artificial" in appearance instead of naturally animated. The child may not laugh or smile unless cued to do so in an appropriate situation, or she may appear to have a collection of rehearsed or "canned" reactions to match certain circumstances.

The child's way of talking may also seem flat and monotone. Her words may sound robotic and carefully measured. Or there may be a lilting tone to her voice, in which her speech sounds as if it's bouncing up and down when she talks.

Your child may have Asperger's Syndrome, or ASD, if she finds it difficult to make friends; doesn't seem to understand nonverbal communications, such as body language or facial expressions; doesn't understand or appears insensitive to others' feelings; is deeply passionate about one or more subject areas; is not physically graceful; has great difficulty accepting change in routine or schedule; or has unusual or mechanical-sounding speech patterns.

Often, the child with Asperger's may find it challenging to demonstrate or understand what others take for granted as a commonsense manner of thought. The child may have a logic all her own that perplexes or exasperates others because it is not representative of the norm. She may not grasp certain social rules or ways of doing things, explained away by others with the phrase "that's the way we do it." Children with Asperger's interpret conversations literally—they have a hard time understanding things like sarcasm, humor, and common sayings.

It is also not uncommon for many children with Asperger's Syndrome to have a desire to maintain order, peace, and tranquility. Your child may (from her logic and perspective) initiate great and creative measures to make others happy and content to maintain the status quo, even if it means making decisions that adults may judge as unwise or unacceptable. It may have more to do with desiring to please in order to keep the peace than with being intuitive to others' needs. For example, the child who breaks into stereotypical stand-up comedian one-liners in order to diffuse what he perceives to be a tense interaction.

Asperger's Syndrome is as unique and individual an experience as each individual is unique. You may find that some, all, or none of the ASD characteristics make sense when you think about your child's way of being in the world.

Prevalence and Misdiagnosis

There has been a great deal of attention given by the media to the skyrocketing increase in the number of children identified with autism. Years ago, it was estimated that 1 in 10,000 individuals was autistic. In the 1990s, the estimate narrowed to 1 in 1,000, then 1 in every 500, then 1 in every 250 children. Data released by the Centers for Disease Control and Prevention in 2014 revised its previous projection of 1 in 110 children to 1 in 68 children, with 1 percent of the world population on the autism spectrum. This rise is occurring without any single known cause or indicator.

Where does this leave our understanding of the prevalence of Asperger's Syndrome? With so much attention being given to young children newly diagnosed with autism, those with milder experiences, or what was known as Asperger's Syndrome, are not usually identified and tracked in the same manner by doctors or our education system. There are a number of reasons for this:

○ One or both parents may have Asperger's Syndrome and do not detect anything out of the ordinary in their child.

○ Families who live in isolated or rural areas, or have limited contact with others with similar-aged, typically developing children, may not recognize their child's differences or may be distanced from proper support systems to obtain a diagnosis.

○ Family practitioners and other physicians may be unaccustomed to identifying the symptoms of autism, let alone understanding Asperger's Syndrome. They may have little to no experience with Asperger's or limited resources from which to gather more information.

○ The child of school age undiagnosed with Asperger's may be labeled as noncompliant or lazy. Parents and teachers may believe she is simply not applying herself to her full potential.

○ The child may be seen as simply quirky or especially gifted, leading to the "Little Professor" moniker that has become a popular way of describing children with Asperger's who present as technically proficient miniature adults.

○ The child may have a diagnosis of hyperlexia, a precocious capacity for reading that far exceeds the child's age; however, the child may be unable to comprehend all that has been read. The child may be fascinated with numbers, may need to keep specific routines, and may be challenged in social interactions.

○ The child could be misdiagnosed with another issue such as a learning disorder, attention deficit disorder, attention deficit hyperactivity disorder, sensory integration disorder, dyslexia, schizophrenia, generalized anxiety disorder, Tourette's Syndrome, obsessive-compulsive disorder, oppositional defiant disorder, bipolar disorder, intermittent explosive disorder, or depression—all mental health experiences listed in the *DSM*.

Like autism, Asperger's knows no social, cultural, or economic boundaries. And, also like autism, it is four times more likely to be found in males than females. Until recently, Asperger's was believed to be largely a male experience, but as our culture is becoming more aware of and better educated to such social issues, more females with Asperger's are being identified.

 **CHAPTER 3**

Seeking Diagnosis

You know your child better than anyone else could. As a conscious parent, you're in tune with his unique personality quirks and behaviors. However, because the symptoms and traits of Asperger's Syndrome can be subtle, even the most focused parents may not recognize any differences in their child until he is age three or older. Pursuing a formal diagnosis is a family's individual decision to make. There are avenues available to aid in this process and a system of community-based and educational services and supports in place to help meet the needs of your child and family.

Is a Diagnosis Necessary?

Each family is unique. The relationships among spouses, children, and extended family can vary drastically. Some families are distant and disconnected from one another. It may be difficult for some family members to outwardly express love and caring. Other families are remarkably and consistently loving and resilient. Still others fall somewhere in between. The dynamics of your family will likely determine how you proceed in seeking a diagnosis of Asperger's Syndrome for your child.

> Your decision to pursue a formal diagnosis is a personalized and individualized decision to make, although many parents agree that they wish to know their child's diagnosis definitively and as early in their child's development as possible so that they can begin advocating for their child and getting him the help he needs.

In observing your child grow and learn, you may have noticed differences in how he is developing when compared with his peers. You may have noticed significant differences in how he interacts with other children. For instance, he may seem not to understand the social rules that other children seem to naturally abide by, such as taking turns in a game. He may play with his toys in ways that are unique but unintended for the toy's purpose, such as dismantling a toy to examine more closely its moving parts. The way he talks may sound overly formal, such as addressing you and your spouse as "mother" and "father" instead of "mommy" and "daddy," or inappropriately calling you by your full first name (e.g., "Susan, please come help me with my bath now"). He may not be as physically graceful as you might wish for him. Or his temper may be prone to escalate when he loses control of his environment.

Perhaps family, friends, or neighbors have brought some of these issues to your attention. They may worry or wonder whether you've witnessed the same differences. When this occurs, it will be important to remember that these people are usually not being nosy, pushy, or humiliating for the sake of making you feel like an inadequate parent. Your concerned family, friends, or neighbors have good reasons for what they're doing, and they are doing the best they know how in the moment. They are merely trying to be helpful in drawing from their own life experiences or those of others they have known. Try listening to their communications and balancing the information they are sharing with what you know to be true.

As a parent, you know your child best. Is there a ring of truth in the collective observations of all? Are others confirming suspicions you've had but suppressed? You see your child every day; the observations of the family member, friend, or neighbor who sees the child less frequently should be weighed carefully, as your child's different way of being may be more apparent to them than to you. Conversely, if neither you nor your spouse is a stay-at-home parent, then you should accept that the observations of your child care or day care professional are similarly made with sincerity. The child care professional can offer you much valuable information about how your child spends his time during the day.

Making the Decision

Most likely, no one at this point will be in a position to suggest Asperger's Syndrome as a viable explanation of your child's way of being. So far, you have some questions and concerns about what you are seeing in your child. A place to start might be to compare what you know to be true of your child's development with the *Diagnostic and Statistical Manual (DSM)* definition of autism spectrum disorder (ASD), which, as of *DSM-5* (published 2013), makes provision for the features of what was Asperger's Syndrome. As you do so, please exercise caution. Specific symptoms in isolation from one another do not a syndrome make.

Say your child has a particularly strong affection for watching the same video every day throughout the day and is interested in watching nothing other than this particular video. This may seem to fall under the category of intense preoccupation with an interest. But if you come up short in checking the remaining diagnostic criteria because your child demonstrates no other symptoms, then he simply has a very strong preference for that one video that may pass once he gets his fill of it.

If you are discovering that the criteria for Asperger's or ASD might have application for your child, then you are faced with a decision about seeking a diagnosis.

The benefits of obtaining a diagnosis may be:

O Being able to put a name and a framework to a collection of symptoms and traits instead of perceiving it all as your child's "bad behavior" or somehow your fault

O Accessing a system of services and supports designed to give your child a head start in life as early as possible

O Being able to educate family, friends, and neighbors about your child's unique way of being when appropriate

O Being able to educate your child about his unique way of being in order to promote self-awareness and self-advocacy, as needed

O Understanding and appreciating sooner your child's lifelong unique qualities, personal needs, and talents

Adults with Asperger's Syndrome who were never diagnosed as children often ask, "Would it have been helpful to have had the diagnosis as a child?" We are still a long way from effectively understanding Asperger's in a concerted, global sense, but having this knowledge early on in the lives of many adults might have aided them to:

O Experience greater success in school

O Be better prepared for higher education, or trade school

O Be better able to initiate and sustain relationships

O Be better equipped to locate viable employment opportunities that best match skills and talents

O Avoid struggles with mental health issues, or be better prepared to care for one's mental health

O Be better prepared to avoid situations in which one may be unwittingly exploited

Local Resources for Diagnosis

If you determine that Asperger's Syndrome or ASD best describes your child's way of being and are interested in pursuing a diagnosis, your first course of action is to seek a referral to the appropriate clinician most qualified to make the diagnosis.

The best place to start is with your child's pediatrician, although she is not in a position to make a diagnosis. You will need to inquire if she knows of a pediatric psychiatrist or psychologist who is experienced in seeing kids with autism spectrum differences. Hopefully the doctor can steer you in the right direction.

If you live in an urban area, there may be a multitude of doctors from which to select. You will need to narrow your range of choices. As autism has become commonplace, you may wish to begin by asking the pediatrician if she can tell you of any other patients who have been pleased with particular diagnosing physicians. The pediatrician may or may not be able to share this information based on client confidentiality or conflict of interest outside of a managed care physician's network.

Finding a doctor experienced in ascertaining an Asperger's Syndrome diagnosis may prove challenging depending upon your geographic location. Search your library or the Internet for statewide and local resources such as established autism groups in your state. They may be helpful in guiding you.

If you live in a rural area, you should still ask your child's pediatrician for a referral, but there's a greater chance that the doctor may not know of anyone who specializes in making autism diagnoses. Or, if the doctor does make a referral, depending upon your location you may have to travel a great distance to access a reputable and established medical center with a pediatric psychiatry department.

PREPARING FOR THE APPOINTMENT

Once you make an appointment with a qualified physician, it is important to be prepared. When setting up the appointment, ask the receptionist or nurse practitioner what kinds of information the doctor expects to receive from you. Is there a form or forms that may be faxed, e-mailed, or mailed to you in advance to save time and ensure a thorough and complete job? Be certain to clarify any insurance concerns you may have as well, and ask how the appointment will be billed. Ask for any information about in-office testing or assessment that may be conducted by the doctor. Is there anything you should be prepared for regarding those tests?

Most often, the doctor will conduct an interview to ask specific questions designed to elicit information about your concerns. Depending upon your child's age, the doctor may wish to meet with your child alone to observe or interview him separately. Find out in advance if that is part of the process. Understand that, because of demand and client backlog, it may be several weeks before a qualified physician has room in his schedule to see you.

Of course, just as you are preparing for this appointment, you will need to help your child to prepare for it as well. Knowledge is power. Your child will do best if he feels safe and comfortable and in control. You may best accomplish this by:

O Explaining that the appointment is with a doctor who only asks questions and does not give shots or ask the child to engage in any other medical-type procedure.

O Sharing with your child your understanding of the structure and sequence of the appointment, including approximate wait time and duration.

O Sharing with your child whatever questions you expect the doctor to ask.

O Going online for a map to show the child exactly where your house is and the route you will take to the doctor's clinic. (Give the child a printout of the map, and partner with him on driving directions while en route the day of the appointment.)

○ Taking your child to the clinic ahead of time to familiarize him with the surroundings and to meet the doctor, if possible. (Take photographs of the building, inside and out, as well as pictures of the doctor and other staff, to give to your child well in advance of the appointment. This preparedness should enhance your child's comfort level.)

○ Empowering the child to mark off the days until the appointment on a prominently displayed wall calendar.

○ Allowing your child to bring a book or small toy related to his most passionate of interests to defer the tedium of waiting before, during, and after the appointment. (The object of passion will also be a terrific icebreaker by which the doctor can initiate conversation with your child.)

These strategies should help you and your child feel fairly comfortable about the impending appointment.

THE DOCTOR'S VISIT

During the appointment, it will be important for you to try to stay as focused as possible and to listen carefully to what the doctor is asking. Often during such a significant time, parents are filled with lots of nervous anxiety, some of which is completely natural. Your anxiety will not be helpful to the doctor if you go overboard. Don't bring stacks of your child's medical, educational, and other records well beyond anything that was requested to show the doctor. Don't digress into lengthy stories intended to highlight one incident in great detail. Be careful not to frequently interrupt in order to further your own preconceived goals such as pressuring the doctor to make an on-the-spot judgment call.

To be helpful to the doctor, bring exactly what was requested. If you bring additional information, offer it only if you think it's warranted or if it helps to illuminate a specific point. Accept that the doctor may not need it at that time. Be prepared to discuss why you believe your child might have Asperger's Syndrome or ASD. Talk about specific clinical symptoms—not behaviors. Tell only concise stories that illustrate your rationale. Allow the doctor to guide the interview, and interject questions only as needed.

By connecting with other parents—either locally, statewide, or nationally—by phone or e-mail, you may receive valuable information about the diagnostic process for your child. Experiences will vary from person to person, but you will surely obtain valuable "pointers" that may help you feel comfortable in knowing what's best to do and say.

It is unlikely that you will walk away from the appointment with an Asperger's Syndrome or ASD diagnosis. The doctor will need time to absorb and process all the information he has gathered from you. A written summary of the meeting and the doctor's observations and findings will be forthcoming. If several weeks go by and you don't receive such a report, contact the clinic to check on its status.

Intervention

There are other avenues to access information on ASD or community services and supports. Every state's county government system has an office that serves infants and children, adolescents, and adults with a variety of different ways of being, covering autism, intellectual impairment, and mental health issues. (The same or a neighboring office may address child welfare, domestic violence issues, and alcohol and substance abuse.) The phone number for your county's local human services office is located in the blue pages of your phone directory, or online at your county's human services website.

THE EARLY INTERVENTION PROGRAM

If your child is younger than five years old, when you call the office, ask for a referral to the Early Intervention Program in order to arrange an assessment of need. Early Intervention is a federally mandated program delivered by every state free of cost to families of children with developmental delays from infancy to school age, or five years old. The Individuals with Disabilities Education Act (IDEA) stipulates the provisions for delivery of Early Intervention.

The Early Intervention office will arrange to have someone come to your home at your convenience to assess your child for developmental delays. If your child qualifies for the program, he may be able to access a variety of professionals and therapists who will educate you about meeting his needs. The challenge in accessing Early Intervention for a child with ASD symptoms that are like Asperger's Syndrome is that the symptoms may be so subtle that kids "fall through the cracks" and go undetected until they are much older than Early Intervention age.

Your child may experience some physical fine- or gross-motor limitations that could make him eligible for the program, and the Early Intervention representative will support you in accessing other local resources that may prove helpful. If your child is blind or deaf, he may also qualify for the program, but the services and supports offered will focus on your child's differences and will likely be unable to address ASD.

Early Intervention is a family-centered program. The intent of the professionals involved is to work directly with you to accommodate your needs, address your concerns, arrange in-person contact according to your schedule, and link you to other people and opportunities that may prove helpful.

However, one area of developmental delay identified for Early Intervention eligibility is social-emotional development, or how well a child relates to others. If your child's social differences are significant enough to cause you concern and he is within Early Intervention age, you may be able to access certain services and support designed to help engage him socially.

HELP FROM SCHOOL

The symptoms of Asperger's Syndrome or ASD may go unnoticed until your child is of school age. If you have been in a "let's wait and see" holding pattern about your child's behaviors, your child's educators may bring it to your attention. They may have noticed your child's distractibility, difficulty in understanding what is expected of him, seeming challenges in social connectedness, and other traits associated with Asperger's. They may recommend a consultation with the school psychologist, who may discuss Asperger's Syndrome or ASD with you.

The school psychologist may assist with observations of your child during the school day or make a referral to a clinician who can make a diagnosis. The school psychologist will then work with the doctor's report to aid the school-based team in supporting your child's social and emotional needs and in making accommodations for your child in the general education curriculum.

Disclosure and Self-Understanding

So the diagnosis has been made. Now what? Once you obtain a diagnosis for your child, you are faced with another significant hurdle: disclosure. With the advent of diagnosis, you will likely be required to interact with others—family, friends, neighbors, doctors, and educators—for the purpose of discussing the diagnosis. You will need to use discretion with disclosure. Please be mindful of being careless of when, how, and with whom you share information, especially if it occurs in your child's presence. Remember, you're talking about your child, and your child is not defined by the diagnosis.

As early as possible, empower your child as the keeper of information. As a conscious parent, you will know best when, where, how, and under what circumstances to broach a discussion about Asperger's Syndrome with your child. You've seen how your child handles receiving information and at what times it is best to approach him. As with any sensitive discussion, you will want to:

- Follow your child's lead by sharing as much or as little information as needed.

- Balance the discussion by highlighting everything you love about your child.

- Underscore that the diagnosis is just a name—nothing else has changed.

- Be prepared to answer any questions your child may have.

- Give your child the opportunity to write, draw, or otherwise make concrete the information as he envisions it.

- Talk about disclosure as the concept of being choosy or very selective about when, where, and with whom personal information is shared.

Regardless of your child's age, he is now your partner in all matters of disclosure. This is a respectful parenting response to supporting the child. This means that prior to arbitrarily sharing personal information about your child's diagnosis, you check with him first to:

- Ask permission to disclose.

- Explain why you believe it is necessary.

- Be open to being flexible if he protests.

- Offer opportunity for compromise.

- Discuss the best, most gentle, most respectful way to disclose the information.

One mother lamented that her child's psychiatrist expects her to disclose sensitive information in front of him, even though her son implores, "No Mom, don't! It's embarrassing!" First, how very fortunate she is that her son is self-aware enough to be a good self-advocate at his young age. There are ways to privately share information that doctors and others require. For example, information may be faxed, mailed, or e-mailed in advance of appointments instead of openly discussing the most humiliating aspects of one's "perceived" behavior so publicly.

Rather than setting aside time for your child to single himself out and reveal his way of being with the entire school class, you may wish to encourage a class discussion of all the students' collective differences and similarities during which your child shares as much or as little as he wishes.

There is power in numbers. If you can establish relationships with other parents, caregivers, and teens and adults with Asperger's Syndrome who are also self-advocates, you can advance the respectful concept of "nothing about me without me." This means that, in a variety of professional and community-based environments, your child has the right to be involved and contribute to all discussions, thus creating positive change in how Asperger's is perceived and discussed by others.

Still, others do select to disclose information as a personal choice. Bonnie's son Noel wrote a wonderful letter to his classmates. Noel has given permission for others to use his letter to adapt for their own use.

I have Asperger's Syndrome, which is on the high end of the autistic spectrum. This means that I experience the world very differently than you do.

You're called "neurologically typical," or "NT," because you don't have ASD. Please don't call me "abnormal" or refer to the other kids as being "normal," because you all seem pretty abnormal to me. I am just not typical because I am wired differently. I like my differences. They give me abilities that most NTs don't have.

People, Communication, and My Interests
Being with lots of people and having conversations that interest you and not me are two things I work very hard at. I don't mean to seem rude when I turn the conversation to my interest. If this is getting in the way, you can tell me that we need to switch topics for a while. I learn best when you relate what you are trying to teach me to one of my interests. I know this might seem strange, but this is just the way

people with an autistic experience are. Relating information to my interests enables me to keep track of many details.

Social skills do not come naturally to me, so I try to keep learning. I usually like to be around adults more than kids, because they are more interesting. I prefer facts over opinions and feelings.

Remember that I don't automatically understand what is going on in terms of verbal and nonverbal communication. People don't always say what they mean, and they use metaphors or a lot of words to say something. This is not how I communicate. I appreciate it when people notice when something doesn't make sense to me and reword it so that I know what they mean. I may not understand what seems very clear to you. Or I may seem rude—although I don't mean to—in the way I speak because I tend to be very direct. Please have patience with me, and explain clearly to me when my way of relating might cause a problem.

Comments like, "Change your attitude" don't help me much. But if you tell me what behavior is bothering you, then I can understand.

Relating to other people is hard work for me. Like other people with autism, I like to have friends, but I also like to be by myself. It is very important that I am allowed to have some "alone time," especially during the times when I am with other people. I try hard to think of other people's feelings and make eye contact, but this doesn't come naturally to me. So could you have a little patience if I come off sounding rude, and explain to me clearly how I could do it better? As long as I am in the mood for it, I try to fit in around people. But this can really wear me out.

Focusing My Thoughts

Sometimes my thoughts come rushing into my head like an avalanche. I'm not sure which one to hold on to, and I might pick the wrong one, which might make you mad.

This happens especially in the morning and at night. If I seem distracted, you can help by giving me only two or three instructions at a time. When this happens, it's better if you come close to me to tell me rather than call to me across the room. Be clear, and remember that my visual and tactile senses are strong, so maybe you can use this to help me. At home I use a lot of pictures and lists to help keep me focused. Remember, I am trying to do my best.

My Sensory Systems

Most people can think of these five senses: hearing, sight, taste, smell, and touch. Did you know that balance and motion are senses, too? My senses often work pretty differently than yours do.

For example, high-pitched and loud sounds, like the singing at church or a vacuum cleaner, really hurt my ears and can be unbearable. I try to have earplugs with me because this helps. Sometimes I'm asked to talk to audiences and they want to clap to show their appreciation. For me it would be better if you would just pat your arm. Thank you.

Like most people with ASD, I tend to think in pictures. I like bright colors like red and orange. If you want me to remember something, it helps if you can show it to me visually. I like to create pictures, watch cartoons, develop visuals on my PC, and play video games.

I don't eat much, and the food has to be mild. Vanilla milkshakes and pumpkin pie are my favorite foods. I like crunchy foods too, like cereal and carrots. When I get thirsty, this sense can be very strong, so I have learned to carry water with me. When I feel stressed or anxious, I've learned that it helps to drink through a straw or eat cereal. Pretty cool, huh?

Tied in with taste is the sense of smell. Strong smells can make me feel sick. Please don't make me eat foods "to be like everyone else," but also, my mom says I should eat as much as I can, and whenever I can when I am in the mood to eat.

Touch, balance, and motion are three senses that really help me when I feel anxious or uncomfortable. A firm touch from you or a place to swing can really help. Sometimes I hang my head upside down or squeeze a ball when the feeling of people around me is too overwhelming.

Routines and Changes

Change can be hard for people with autism. Some warning or explanation before a new activity helps me a lot. Also, transitions are easier if I am given the schedule ahead of time. It helps me to have it written down so that I can see it.

Time is a strange concept for me. When I'm bored, time seems to go by twice as slow as a snail. But when I am doing something I like, it goes twice as fast as a cheetah. Try to understand that I don't experience time the same way you do.

In Conclusion

Someday I hope to use my knowledge and abilities to invent things that will really help people. Did you know that people like Albert Einstein, Thomas Jefferson, and Marie Curie had Asperger's? Many people think that Bill Gates does, too. I hope to be the next in line of these great scientists and thinkers.

Sometimes I get frustrated because I have to work so hard to fit in and conform to your way of being. But I like myself. God has been good to me by giving me a nice family and letting me be smart. I hope that what I do in the future with my special gifts benefits you someday.

Thank you for your patience and for taking the time to read this. I hope you will be my friend.

Sincerely,
Noel

Important Points to Consider

Seeking a diagnosis is truly a family decision. If your child is young you may make this decision on your own with your child's best interests in mind. However, if your child is old enough, have an open discussion with your child about what getting a diagnosis would involve and what it could mean for your child if he does receive a diagnosis of Asperger's Syndrome.

If you and your child do seek a diagnosis, keep these points in mind:

○ A diagnosis does not change your child. He is still intrinsically who he is as a person. A diagnosis is not a label that will identify your child for the rest of his life.

○ A diagnosis can open up the door to receiving help and support at school and through support groups where your child can meet other people he can identify with.

○ Before visiting a specialist, make sure your child is as aware as possible about what the appointment will be like. This may mean visiting the office ahead of the appointment day so your child will be familiar with it, marking the day of the visit on a calendar so your child can feel prepared, and allowing your child to bring a comfort object.

○ If your child does receive a diagnosis, be respectful of your child's wishes about sharing it with others.

As always be prepared to be a sounding board for your child's concerns and questions. A diagnosis can be intimidating and may raise some fears for your child. Educating yourself on this condition will make you a better resource for your child when he needs your compassion and support.

CHAPTER 4

Discipline

As a conscious parent, you tend to take a nonjudgmental, empathetic approach to discipline rather than the fear-based techniques of traditional parenting. But that doesn't mean you don't set limits or ignore bad behaviors in your children. Keep in mind, though, that disciplining the child with Asperger's Syndrome or ASD requires some finesse in balancing a number of considerations. You have the right to set the same limitations and boundaries as you would for any of your children. But you also have the responsibility to clearly communicate your rules to the child with Asperger's in ways she understands best. Only then can you expect her compliance, within reason, and apply discipline fairly.

Benbrook Public Library

Your Approach to Discipline

All parents are faced with the task of child rearing to the best of their ability. Loving your child as you do, you want to know you're doing the right thing. Because each child is a unique individual, there is no single method for raising your specific child, only sound generalizations for you to test and apply. Your approach to disciplining your child will likely draw from several sources, including your memories of how you were disciplined as a child; strategies, philosophies, and ideas you've read and with which you concur; and personal observations of how your family, friends, and neighbors discipline their own children.

The key to disciplining your child with Asperger's Syndrome is to—first and foremost—recall the positive philosophies discussed in Chapter 1:

O Your child has good reasons for doing what she's doing.

O She's doing the very best she knows how to in the moment (and with what she's got available to her).

O She needs to feel safe and comfortable and in control.

O She will become unhinged by anything significantly unpredictable.

You know your child best. She may be a very sensitive individual, but you have the right as a parent to set realistic expectations of obligations and responsibilities as you would for any other child.

Your child's need to feel in control should not be taken to extremes. Parents must set limits and expectations for all children. Having Asperger's Syndrome does not give one free rein to be out of control; after all, you wouldn't allow your other children to do everything they want, whenever they please. Before you react, however, you will also need to be mindful that your children's logic will not necessarily reflect your idea of common sense. For example, imagine a teenager who is driving down the highway and sees a box in the middle of the road. He decides the box must be empty and drives over it, rather than around it. The box isn't empty and damages his car. Even though his logic is questionable, he did not deliberately attempt to damage the car.

Setting Rules

Many parents assume that a child should understand appropriate social behavior under a wide variety of specific circumstances, and when that doesn't occur, they can react with anger in the heat of the moment.

For example, suppose you are in attendance at a wedding and your child with Asperger's is bored or distracted. To your chagrin, she insists on telling everyone around her the flight schedule of every major airline departing from your local airport in a loud, clear voice that carries. Your first reaction may be to "shush" her into silence. When that proves ineffective, you may firmly whisper to her to stop. When that doesn't work, you may take hold of her and make a threat, such as the loss of a reward, special privilege, or favored plaything. As a last resort, you may physically remove her from the setting. You intervened when the situation required it.

However, as the parent of a child with Asperger's Syndrome, your approach to discipline should be one of prevention, not intervention.

> Conscious parenting may draw upon all your sleuthing skills in discerning the truth when it comes to discipline. Don't be deceived by first impressions of a situation by readily jumping to the conclusion that your child has made a serious error in judgment. Give her time to explain. Was her motive altruistic (though way off base), or was she trying to protect someone else?

Your child with Asperger's Syndrome can know only what she knows. Many children with Asperger's interpret information in ways that are very literal and concrete. Remember Tom Hanks as the boy in a man's body in the movie *Big*? At a reception, he drew stares and raised eyebrows by attempting to eat the miniature corn as he would regular corn on the cob. He wasn't trying to be socially inappropriate on purpose. Never having had experience with the social conventions of consuming the mini hors d'oeuvres, he was doing his best in the moment.

Like the parent in the wedding scenario, you may expect your child to automatically "read" your body language and facial expressions of displeasure or to transfer what she's learned in a similar environment to the present situation. It doesn't usually work that way. Most important, your child is not consistently misbehaving solely for the sake of "being bad."

Communicating Expectations

In all matters of disciplining the child with Asperger's Syndrome, you have the responsibility to be fair in how you communicate rules and expectations. Because your child will be most open to receiving this information in ways that are literal and concrete, you should make the information tangible. That is, put it in writing as a simple bullet-point list. It may even be a partnered agreement that you both review and sign together. This will provide your child with a personal investment in the agreement and give her an incentive to comply. The list of rules becomes your child's property and, depending upon the situation, should be kept in her pocket for ready reference. Be open and flexible enough to listen to her questions; she is not challenging you, merely in need of clarification of what you're trying to communicate.

Numbering each item on the list may aid your child's recall. You may even wish to decide, in partnership with your child, how many warnings she'll get to stop breaking the rules before you implement your standard means of discipline.

To revisit the earlier wedding scenario, with such an agreement both you and your child are well prepared as to your expectations (and those dictated by the environment) prior to going into the situation. Not only is this fair, it is prevention, not intervention.

A sample list of rules for the wedding scenario might look like this:

RULES FOR GOING TO A WEDDING

O Before the service begins, it is okay to talk with other people, especially people I know.

- When everyone is sitting down, people will usually be very quiet or whisper. Everyone expects me to be quiet or to whisper, too.

- If I am not being quiet or if I am whispering too much, Mom or Dad (or spouse) will tell me about it and ask me to stop. They will do this because I am distracting other people who want to see and hear the service.

- If I get bored during the service, I will think about something else, quietly draw or read, or play a silent game I bring with me.

- When the service ends and people get up, it is okay to talk in my normal voice again.

When preparing to leave for the wedding, remind your child to bring the rules along (unless she is able to use photographic memory and recite them by rote). On the drive there, review the rules together. When you notice your child becoming restless during the service, she may need reminders about the alternatives you both agreed to. If your child requires a warning, remind her of the rules and why she's getting the warning. You can use this positive strategy in numerous and similar social circumstances.

If your child continues to behave improperly, it may be appropriate to discipline at this time. The operative word here is "may," and to further complicate things, there might be mitigating factors to dissuade you from discipline in the moment. These factors will be discussed at the end of this chapter.

The ability to "call up" visual information at will does not necessarily mean that your child can do this at your command. You may find this confusing if she can, for instance, recite, on cue, intricate details relative to her most passionate interests but be unable to "replay" concepts you've impressed upon her. Like all kids, your child may need visual reminders and practice to get it down.

Seeing Your Child's Point of View

Again, never assume your child will automatically transfer and apply information previously learned in one environment to a new situation that, in your mind, is remarkably similar. For that child, a new situation is a new situation.

Consider this example: A teenage boy with Asperger's once decided to drive his family's car while his parents were out. His family was preparing to junk the car and had let the insurance on it expire. The young man knew this but took the car out anyway. He believed the worst that might happen would be getting into a minor fender bender and being held responsible for paying the damage costs, as had been his previous experience with car accidents. When he arrived home, his very upset parents confronted him. They were distraught over the implications of driving without insurance—the potential for a major collision that could've involved serious damage, injury, or death to others and for which they would be held personally responsible. The teenager had no idea of these potential ramifications of his actions. If he had, he likely would not have entertained the notion of taking the car anywhere.

As previously acknowledged, your child with Asperger's Syndrome is likely to be very emotionally sensitive. She may tear up and weep at song lyrics or commercials. She may be unable to keep from dwelling on a particularly disturbing news story. Given this, it's important that you never make idle threats in anger or exasperation that have finality to their tone, such as, "I wish you'd just disappear!"

If you are going through a time where you find yourself short on patience and prone to irrational outbursts, be prepared for your child to withdraw from you more and more until you are shut out completely. Other fear-based techniques such as spanking, slapping, hitting, or grabbing will produce results equally as damaging.

As a conscious parent, you do your best to keep sarcastic comments and comments made in the heat of anger out of your interactions with your child, but all parents are human, and all people say things they don't mean on occasion. However, saying anything along these lines to the child with Asperger's Syndrome will have a long-lasting, damaging effect, possibly for the duration of her life. Why? Because, quite simply, she will believe every word of what you're saying as the truth. This will cause undue anxiety, stress, and upset that will persist over time. Your child may take personally criticisms you think mild or trivial. She may cry, pout, or sulk for hours or longer.

Knowing When to Discipline

Knowing when, how, and how much to discipline your child with Asperger's Syndrome can be quite challenging. You may be filled with worry for your child and her future. You may be learning more about becoming her strongest advocate. In so doing, you will need to find balance in your role as a parent and disciplinarian. There may be a fine line between being an effective parent and being perceived as zealous or coddling of your child.

Remember that kids are kids. You would never do anything to intentionally endanger your child; but, as much as you might wish to keep all your children safe from any harm or wrongdoing, sometimes life's most valuable (and enduring) lessons come courtesy of that famous institution of learning and life experience known as the school of hard knocks.

Your child's diagnosis describes a sliver of who she is as a human being. She is many other things; her diagnosis does not exclusively define her (remember the self-fulfilling prophecy). In valuing your child's gifts and talents concurrent with understanding her diagnosis, be cautious about going to extremes. You have every reason to be a strong advocate on behalf of your child and in protection of her rights. But this does not exempt her from being disciplined by you or, where appropriate, by child care or day care providers, or educators.

OVERPROTECTIVENESS

Some parents can become overprotective. They may make frequent excuses for their child's words or actions. And they may not discipline where most others agree it to be warranted. When this occurs—regardless of the child's way of being—the balance of authority shifts. The child gains more and more control while being protected in a sheltered environment with little to no discipline.

The Latin root of the word "discipline" means "to teach." Parents who are overprotective and do nothing to discipline their child are teaching some very artificial life lessons that will significantly hinder their child in the real world. One mother openly despaired that she envisions caring for her son with Asperger's Syndrome for the rest of her life. This may indeed be the case if she micromanages every aspect of his life.

THE DIGNITY OF RISK

There is what is known as the "dignity of risk." It speaks to the luxury you must allow people with different ways of being to make long- and short-term mistakes—but with support and guidance. This will be a great challenge to you as a parent who is naturally protective of your child. But it is the only way your child will learn and prepare for greater independence in the future. Disciplining your child should be a teaching and learning opportunity about making choices and decisions. When your child makes mistakes, assure her that she is still loved and valued. In other words, focus on the issue at hand, not the person (e.g., yelling "How could you be so stupid?" is not an option).

For example, the parents of the teenager who drove the uninsured car should demonstrate their discipline by first discussing his great error in judgment in addition to entering into a dialogue about good, better, and best choices in the future. It will be especially helpful—and will maximize the learning opportunity—if, in partnership with the boy, they write it all down to make it as concrete as possible. They may also decide that another form of discipline (such as withholding allowance or grounding him) is an entirely appropriate way to reinforce the seriousness of his actions.

This is not to suggest that they should not have intervened if they had had prior knowledge of his intentions; they certainly should have! But, where possible, look for small opportunities to deliberately allow your child to mess up and make mistakes for which you can set aside discipline-teaching time. It will be a learning process for you and your child.

Meltdowns

Earlier, during discussion of the wedding scenario, it was stated, "If your child continues to behave improperly, it may be appropriate to discipline at this time." The word "may" was emphasized. In addition to being certain that you are communicating your limitations and expectations in as direct, clear, and concrete a way as possible, you will have to take into consideration three other areas before you discipline.

Think of the variety of things that parents and others consider "bad behaviors" in all kids, and especially in kids with Asperger's Syndrome or autism. These behaviors include:

- Hitting
- Kicking
- Spitting
- Biting
- Pulling hair
- Scratching
- Swearing
- Smearing or throwing feces
- Urinating in places other than the toilet
- Physically harming others, including loved ones
- Damaging property
- Doing harm to oneself

Some of these behaviors are seen from time to time in all kids. Still others are quite extreme, like property damage or self-harm. In isolation, these actions may be rarities. When they happen consistently, they become red flags of a serious nature because it is very unusual for these activities to occur consistently for any child. Let's call these behaviors "junk."

It is important to recognize that these junk behaviors are not "behaviors" but communications.

THREE MELTDOWN TRIGGERS

The inability to communicate—to articulately express oneself—in ways that are effective, reliable, and universally understandable is the first meltdown trigger. The other two meltdown triggers fall under the umbrella of communications as well.

The second meltdown trigger is pain and discomfort. That is, severe physical pain and discomfort that is not being communicated in ways that are effective, reliable, and universally understandable.

The third meltdown trigger is mental health issues. That is, significant mental health experiences that are not being communicated in effective, reliable, and universally understandable ways.

The latter two areas fall under the communication umbrella because communication is everything. If you cannot express your physical or mental pain in the moment, then that obstacle is a communication issue. One or any combination of these three areas—communication, pain, or mental health—is what drives the junk behaviors, not Asperger's Syndrome. That's the good news. If you've succumbed to believing stereotypes about Asperger's, then this revelation may come as a surprise to you. Simply because your child has Asperger's, it does not follow that she will automatically manifest some or all of the junk behaviors as a direct result of Asperger's. This is an untruth; otherwise, such behaviors would be listed as ASD criteria in the *DSM*. Because your child is inherently gentle and exquisitely sensitive, she may be particularly prone to being vulnerable; she may be more susceptible than neurotypical individuals to experiencing issues of communication, pain, and mental health.

DEALING WITH THE MELTDOWN AREAS

But these vulnerabilities are not directly affiliated with the diagnosis of Asperger's Syndrome or ASD. They are byproducts of the ASD experience in some—not all—children. The three meltdown-trigger areas—communication, pain and discomfort, and mental health issues—are of great importance and will be explored in detail in this book. In order to be an effective parent and disciplinarian of a child with Asperger's Syndrome, you will need to comprehend these areas fully and place them in the proper context of any given situation. This knowledge will aid you in laying a foundation for prevention in order to minimize your intervention.

All the resources of your parenting wisdom and expertise may be needed in making respectful speculations about what might be driving a meltdown. Your child may find it extremely difficult or impossible to clearly articulate all the factors that came to bear upon her loss of control. By taking a mindful parenting approach, think about the last time you experienced extreme distress or anger—in hindsight, were you similarly challenged and able to express your motivators?

Important Points to Consider

You need to set limits and expectations for your child with Asperger's Syndrome just as you would for any of your children. However, you will need to keep some points in mind in order to discipline your child fairly:

O Your child should be made aware of what exactly is expected of her in a situation. Many parents find that having an actual physical list of expected behaviors makes it easier for their children to understand what is expected of them.

O Discipline for your child with Asperger's should always aim for prevention rather than intervention.

O Before disciplining your child, stop and try to see the situation from her point of view.

○ Be mindful of circumstances that may increase the likelihood of undesirable behavior from your child (meltdown triggers) and try to avoid those situations where possible. If you can't avoid them, place them in the appropriate context when disciplining your child. For example, did she do the best she could given the situation?

○ Focus on the issue, not the person. Your child should know that she is loved but her action is not appropriate.

○ Allow your child the "dignity of risk." Within reason, allow your child to make her own choices.

 **CHAPTER 5**

Communication

Communication is key to being empathetic and tolerant in a conflict. However, as an individual with Asperger's Syndrome, one of your child's greatest challenges is in the area of communication. It will be important to grasp how you can communicate in ways that will support your child's ease of understanding. It will be equally important to comprehend how best to assist him in deciphering communication in everyday conversation. Your child wants to be socially accepted by his peers, and your efforts to foster a mutual comfort level where communication is concerned will be paramount.

How Would You Feel?

The last chapter discussed the three meltdown triggers that typically drive "behaviors" in children with ASD. You will recall that the most significant of those three areas was the inability to communicate in ways that are effective, reliable, and universally understandable. When you are feeling overwhelmed by circumstances that are unpredictable and that spiral out of your control, you may find it very difficult to verbally express yourself in this situation. For example, think how you would feel if, all in the same morning:

O You oversleep because the alarm didn't go off.

O You have no hot water for a shower.

O You realize you're out of coffee.

O You don't notice that your pants have an obvious fabric snag until you're in the car.

O The entrance to your freeway exit is detoured due to construction.

O You can't find a parking space at work.

When you finally get inside your workplace, you are likely feeling one or all of the following:

O Angry

O Upset

O Disoriented

O Short-tempered

O Depressed

O Anxious

O Stressed

Upon your arrival at work, what do you instinctively want to do? Find a friend or confidante as soon as possible in order to vent and tell them about your morning. But where would you start? If you are feeling emotionally stressed or overwhelmed, you may be feeling like a huge, confused mass of all the feelings listed. You may not have the words to describe your frustration, or you may be completely inarticulate in the moment. If you can't get it all out in a way that is effective, reliable, and universally understandable, your frustration will continue to build. Now suppose someone unaware of your experience approaches you and makes a demand that is time-sensitive ("I need this within a half hour!"). Everything you're feeling will escalate until you release it in some way. You may do this by:

- Yelling or screaming

- Swearing

- Throwing something

- Breaking something

- Pulling something off the wall

- Clearing off your desk with a sweep of your arm

- Sitting and crying

- Avoiding the situation by disappearing to the bathroom, lounge, or smoking area

- Going numb and not responding to anything

Fortunately, such overwhelming experiences are rarities for most people. But isn't it curious how many of these reactive behaviors are similar to the list of Asperger's Syndrome "junk behaviors" outlined in the last chapter? If anyone accused you of being unprofessional or even violent in manifesting such behaviors, wouldn't you defend yourself by explaining they were communications of your tremendous angst, and that you were coping the best way you knew how? This scenario played out over the course of a few hours one morning. But you may use it as an analogy to understand how most kids with Asperger's feel every day when trying to cope with events while navigating communication.

Mindful parenting when your child is overwhelmed means simply abandoning all expectations of trying to understand in favor of being present in the moment of now: providing a gentle hug or allowing your child to have a good cry or personal space to temporarily shut down. Providing these unspoken communications may have as much impact as your verbal communications in the moment, or perhaps more.

Your child may be quite challenged in his ability to process receptive language, that is, understand what others are communicating. You may be frustrated by his apparent unawareness of the social repercussions of interrupting or saying something with brutal directness. Conversely, his idea of communication to others, or expressive language, may be skewed from what is considered the norm. Let's examine both perspectives.

Communicating Visually

It is important to understand how your child with Asperger's Syndrome thinks and processes information. According to a number of self-advocates with Asperger's, many individuals with Asperger's are visual thinkers. This means, quite literally, that they think in constant streams of images and movies—not Hollywood movies, but life-event "memory" movies. This way of thinking is very different from most others. You may think in pictures too, perhaps more so if someone specifically directs you to do so by saying "Picture this" or "Imagine this." It may be an unnatural way of thinking for you without putting forth great effort, but it is a flowing, seamless, and natural manner of thought for many people with Asperger's or even autism.

If you were to think exclusively in imagery, and you were in conversation with someone, then you'd likely require some processing time to mentally "call up" pictures and movies based upon your life experiences in order to follow what the person is saying. If you are discussing something relatively familiar or even appealing, then the flow of pictures may be

As a fun little role-reversal exercise, set aside time for a game with your child. Request that he read the rules to his favorite video or computer game (or some other element related to his passions). Ask that he read up to four paragraphs, plowing right through without pause, while you listen silently. Once he is finished, *you* draw exactly what he has described and see how close you get in accuracy. It may be eye-opening for you, and should cause you to appreciate his need for processing time the next time you give him a list of *verbal* instructions!

effortless. But what if your communication partner is relating new information for which you have no prior knowledge or experience? You would have to be especially attentive and try to listen very carefully to make sure you understood clearly. Concurrently, you would be attempting to call up or form mental images to equate what you think the person is telling you (which is perfectly obvious to them).

Extra Processing Time

What if you are a child with Asperger's and your communication partner is your parent or other adult in authority? If the adult doesn't "get" the way you think, you will be set up for failure when given multipart, verbal instruction. As a society, people have been conditioned to communicate with lightning-fast speed and to expect the same in return. But the child with Asperger's will need processing time to catalog the sequence of steps being communicated and make a facsimile image or movie of each that most closely approximates what he thinks the adult is trying to say.

If you're communicating something new and different to the child, then assimilating the information and translating it into images and movies will take time. Your challenge as a parent is to slow down and carefully measure the amount of information dispensed to avoid confusion. If your child is unable to visualize what you verbally communicate, he is less likely to retain it.

You've experienced something similar when you've been lost and stopped to ask for directions. You may have quickly learned that you asked for more than you bargained for if the person who gave you directions slowly built, layered, and embellished the information until you could not keep track of the list of verbal information. Apply this scenario to the child with Asperger's Syndrome and you can understand how easy it would be to blame his inability to correctly follow through on noncompliance, or "bad" behavior.

Because your child may be a pleaser or have a flat affect, you may be unable to tell through body language or facial expressions whether he understands—even if he says he does. If you wish to be certain you are communicating in ways that are effective, reliable, and universally understandable, take a few moments and go through these steps:

O Rethink what you intend to communicate. Can it be simplified?

O Before giving your child instruction, ask him to prepare to make pictures or movies of what you're conveying. Check back on this during your communication by saying something like "Can you see it?" or "Do you see what that's supposed to look like?"

O Slow the pace of your instruction—especially if it's about something new and different.

O Allow for processing time in between steps of instruction. Given how you've been conditioned to interact with others, this will be tough to do, but necessary.

O Ask your child if he's ready for more.

O After you've finished talking, give your child a chance to ask clarifying questions.

O Ensure your child's understanding of what you've communicated by asking him to describe what you've just said, or, if it's easier for him, writing or typing the instructions.

Be cautious about overloading your child with too much information all in one shot. As your child's parent, you will be able to best gauge how much or how little he can absorb at once.

Eye Contact

Be advised that many children with ASD will not be as successful as they could be when given instruction if they are required to make direct eye contact concurrent with your delivery of instruction. You may recall your own parents commanding direct eye contact by saying something to the effect of "Look at me when I'm talking to you." Society has ingrained the belief that if you make direct eye contact in conversation, you are listening carefully and paying close attention. The twist is that for the child with Asperger's Syndrome, the opposite may very well be true.

> In some cultures it is a show of respect not to make eye contact while in conversation with others. The next time someone does not make direct eye contact with you, try to pay attention to the thoughts that enter your mind. You may find that some or all of your negative thoughts are socially conditioned.

The child with Asperger's who is across the room from you and appears not to be listening may be taking in nearly everything—if not quite everything—you are saying, as opposed to the child who is compelled to make direct eye contact to "prove" he is paying attention. Why would this be so? Remember that your child is likely extremely visual in how he assimilates and absorbs information. When you speak, your face is in constant motion and there are many, many visual distractions, such as your eyes and glasses, your hair, your jewelry, your mouth, saliva, tongue, and teeth, and your clothing, not to mention other contributing factors such as your breath and cologne.

Your child will be tremendously challenged to pay attention and listen if he is distracted by one, some, or all of these visual details. He will be faced with complying with the social expectation of making direct eye contact every day outside his own home. Reflect carefully upon your ability to be flexible where direct eye contact is concerned, especially when giving directions. Your child may surprise you. If you feel that direct eye contact is nonnegotiable in your family, then find compromise in:

- Seeking opportunities to make direct eye contact attractive or appealing, such as holding some favored item up near your face, while requesting eye contact.

- Accepting your child's need to make fleeting eye contact, look away, then look back.

- Accepting your child's "ballpark" approximation of direct eye contact if he stares at your ears, mouth, or some area of your face other than your eyes while you are talking.

- Accepting your child's need to look away from your eyes in order to formulate a thoughtful, articulate response.

Creating Trust

Your child may be very dependable. That is, he does what he says he's going to do when he says he's going to do it. Because your child likely interprets others' communications in a very literal sense, he will expect you to do the same. In communicating with your child, it will be important that you do what you say you're going to do by keeping your promises—you'll be held to it! If you consistently overlook, cover up, or excuse your broken promises, you are chipping away at any trust your child has placed in you, and your relationship will grow ever distant.

The child with Asperger's says what he means and means what he says with the same definitiveness. That is, no means no and yes means yes. Your child's anxiety and frustration will likely escalate if you repeatedly ask the same question or ask him to change his mind without explanation.

Conscious parenting requires that you apologize to your child as soon as possible after breaking a promise. Let him know precisely when you will fix the situation or make it right. If you approach such interactions in this respectful manner—and follow through as you said you would—your chances of being forgiven are far greater than if you do nothing.

Helping Your Child Crack the "Social Code"

Now that you've read about the way your child will best receive information, let's explore how he may best express communication. As you've just learned, your child may be very literal in his way of being and in everything he does and says. Part of his challenge in making sense of social interactions is to assume some flexibility and understanding when others are not as rigid.

CASUAL PROMISES THAT CONFUSE

People commonly make promises they have absolutely no intention of keeping. People say things all the time that sound friendly and sincere—and they may be genuine in the moment—but they get distracted, forget, or get involved in other things and never follow through. Some of these popular idioms include such catch phrases as "I'll call you in a few days," "Let's do lunch real soon," or "I'll stop by to see you in a couple of weeks." They haven't intentionally misled you, and most people shrug them off when these social dates don't come to fruition if they haven't already interpreted them as weightless social conventions. The phrases are spoken in the same spirit as asking, by rote, "How are you?" without really expecting to hear a rundown of how someone actually is.

Meanwhile, the person with Asperger's is waiting for the other party to come through and make good on the promise. With each day that passes with no communication, the person becomes more hurt, confused, or upset. Some folks probably forget making such comments as soon as they say them, or would be a bit surprised to be held closely accountable for them. You will need to counsel your child in this peculiar nuance of neurotypical behavior, especially as he enters his teen years— a time when people rely less on their parents and interact with greater social freedom.

Subtleties of Language

Another great challenge your child may grapple with is in understanding the flow of typical, everyday conversations. The language most people are accustomed to using may get "lost" on the child with Asperger's Syndrome. This is because everyday interactions are peppered with subtleties, including:

○ Slang (Example: "He lost his head!")

○ Sarcasm (Example: "You're such a hottie!" but meaning just the opposite.)

○ Innuendo (Example: "They slept together last weekend.")

○ Irony (Example: "Be sharp or you'll be flat.")

Most people learn to understand these subtleties by osmosis—simply by experiencing a reasonably typical upbringing in which they've automatically inferred meaning into previously unfamiliar idioms. They use body language and other cues to interpret the real meaning of the words. Many children with Asperger's are not privy to this "social code" and require your gentle coaching to decipher it.

We all occasionally need such clarifications because we are all more alike than different. For instance, if someone said to you, "Duck," would you know how to interpret it? Would you look around for a bird, or would you physically lower your head to avoid being hit by something? Based on your past experience, the chances of being struck might seem higher than your chances of seeing the bird, and therefore you might "duck" your head. But it was a split-second judgment call.

Here are two different real-life scenarios involving boys with Asperger's that illustrate how slang is frequently misinterpreted. In the first situation, a mother kept her distance in observing her young son's interaction with a baker when placing the order for his birthday cake. The boy responded well to questions such as, "What flavor icing would you like?" and "What flavor cake would you like?" But when the baker asked, "And what would you like your cake to say?" the very surprised boy exclaimed, "Are you crazy? Cakes don't talk!" In a worst-case scenario, one boy became a target for some older boys at summer camp. One of them told him to go jump in a lake—so he did, fully clothed. The boy jumped into the lake because:

○ The other boy was older and perceived as intimidating or in authority, so the boy did as he was told (being a "pleaser")

○ There was a lake there so it didn't occur to the boy that his tormentor could be referring to anything other than that lake

○ He was unaware of the slang expression that means the same as "Buzz off" or "Get lost"

These expressions will need to be taught to the child with Asperger's. As an exercise, you may wish to sit with your child and develop a list of words and phrases that draw inspiration from the previous list of subtleties in language. It will be helpful if you are prepared to give examples for each item on the list. Your child will be greatly amused if you are able to share your own experiences of misunderstanding someone's meaning and intent, and ask your child to provide his thoughts about what you might've done differently, or how you would know better next time. When discussed as a "game" in this manner—and outside of real-life, potentially threatening, or scary situations—your child will likely feel comfortable and at ease deconstructing social idioms. Reinforce that it is always considered acceptable to politely request that someone repeat what they've said, or ask for clarification by simply stating, "I don't know what you mean. Can you please say it another way?" By doing this, you can help your child become adept at cracking the social code.

Texting—A Good Thing?

In today's world it is the rare adult who does not use a cell phone. Rarer still is the child or teen without a cell phone of his own. Your decision to obtain a cell phone for your child with Asperger's was likely motivated by his request (or insistence!) and your desire for the ability to be in close contact when apart. Cell phones have become increasingly sophisticated as technology advances, and text messaging is part and parcel of cell phone ownership. But is this a good thing where your child is concerned? The answer may be mixed. Is your child well-versed enough in cracking the social code so that text messages—with all the slang, abbreviations, and shorthand—are understood true to their intent? Is your child at risk for being bullied or coerced via text messaging? In addition to text messaging ("texting"), photos and videos can also be easily sent between users. Because of this ease, much attention has been given to "sexting" or the transmission of nude or seminude images of young people with or without their consent. If your child has strong social connections, this may be a nonissue. But if your child has experienced social difficulties, is he also at risk for being used as a "patsy" or the person set up to take the blame under such circumstances? Would he willingly participate under the guise of social acceptance?

On the other hand, because texting does not require face-to-face interaction in which eye contact is expected, communicating in this way may make your child's differences less apparent. In addition to thoroughly educating your child about the dos and don'ts of cell phone use, the following section may aid you in navigating both spoken *and* written social interactions.

Additional Social Strategies

It is easy for your child to misunderstand communications and do something other than you intended, or react with frustration when he tries and fails. Your child may be additionally challenged when interacting with peers and others because he:

- O Has difficulty understanding the rhythmic flow of conversation (i.e., the reciprocation, or "give and take")

- O Talks off topic or interjects information that doesn't fit the moment

- O Is direct and honest and, in so being, is offensive to others

- O Doesn't understand how to maintain personal space

- O Has trouble deciphering people's body language

There are a number of concrete strategies you may explore to address such issues.

DEBRIEFING

Try debriefing social situations that were confusing or upsetting by privately, gently, and respectfully deconstructing them portion by portion. Request your child to model his recall of others' body language and facial expressions, or model them yourself and ask, "Is this what you saw?" Once you identify the breakdown in communication, you can better explain what transpired. You may wish to take the subtle language that was originally confusing and exaggerate it in an obvious way. Once your child "sees" it, talk about the less-exaggerated communication originally used.

Carol Gray, a special educator, has developed Comic Strip Conversations, a wonderful, visual technique whereby you and your child draw—comic-strip style—social conversations using voice balloons to contain dialogue. Gray encourages using a color-coding system to identify emotions for further clarification. Many kids with Asperger's enjoy drawing, and this strategy is a safe and comfortable way to give your child control in deconstructing social misunderstandings or ideas to apply in the future. It is also a visual way to show turn-taking in conversation, approximate comfort-zone distance from others, and how people's conversations can become jumbled and overlap when someone interrupts too frequently or disrupts the flow by talking off topic.

MAKING LISTS OR VIDEOS

Develop a written list of key phrases that your child can use as a socially acceptable entry into conversation. There can be a hierarchy in the sequence of phrases such that they may flow into broader, larger conversations, such as "Hey, what's up?" "What's new with you?" "What did you do over the weekend?" "What did you watch on TV last night?" These questions also promote turn-taking that includes eye contact (where possible). If your child gets stuck, he may also fall back on using typical "scripted" but kid-acceptable responses such as "Cool" or "That's awesome."

You may also wish to consider videotaping. The caution here is that no one sees and hears himself as others do, and it can be quite disturbing for anyone to watch himself on video. If you wish to try it, ensure that you have your child's permission. It may also be helpful not to single out your child but to naturally capture him engaged in some activities with others. Be certain that any debriefing you do with your child occurs in a gentle, accepting environment. This was the case for one teenage boy videotaped during a discussion group at school. When he privately viewed the video, he was astounded that he came across differently than his perception of himself, and after that he worked to tame and refine his presentation style.

To support your child using video to deconstruct his social interactions, do it as naturally as possible. If your child knows you are singling him out, he may "overact" and play to the camera. Try videoing at family gatherings or picnics, at parties, while playing games, or during other activities. Always watch the video with your child in privacy.

WRITING

Many people are better at expressing themselves in writing than through oral communication. Here is where computers are a tremendous benefit to kids with Asperger's. The computer is liberating because your child is free from social pressures with regard to immediacy of response, body language, facial expressions, personal space issues, and eye contact in conversation. With e-mail, you can respond in your own time. You may be amazed at the incredible and eloquent insights your child types out in his own time and in the safety and comfort of his own home.

Many kids with Asperger's feel so socially inept that in-person "talk therapy" or group counseling is often ineffective. Try reaching your child with pressing questions and concerns by sending him an e-mail; you will get a reply that may surprise and enlighten your own understanding of the situation at hand.

If your child is receiving formal supports from your county's service system or your school district, you may wish to encourage the professionals with whom your child interacts to pursue these and other strategies of effective communication. They should be in a position to do so, or may already be knowledgeable about them.

Important Points to Consider

As a conscious parent, you are already aware of the importance of communication with your child. You try to keep an open dialogue with your child and are aware of his unique issues when it comes to communicating. Issues may arise, however, as your child has to communicate with peers at school or others in the outside world. To aid your child in communication skills, keep the following things in mind:

○ Create trust with your child by doing what you say you will do. And if you don't or can't follow through, apologize to your child and remedy the situation.

○ Relinquish the need for eye contact from your child. Eye contact can often lead to distraction and confusion in children with Asperger's, and they can often listen better to you if they are not forced to look directly at you.

○ Periodically review subtleties in language with your child (such as sarcasm, innuendo, and so on) so when he encounters them in social conversations he will not be confused.

○ Share your personal stories of miscommunication with your child. Not only will this give your child a laugh, it will also reassure him that everyone make mistakes in interpretation and will help with any self-esteem issues he may have about communication mistakes he has made.

○ Help your child discover other avenues of communication that he may excel in. Perhaps he can write, draw, or make videos to express himself more effectively.

 **CHAPTER 6**

Mental Health

As an inherently gentle and exquisitely sensitive being, your child may be particularly vulnerable to mental health problems. Such experiences transpire in people with Asperger's Syndrome more often than not. As a conscious parent, your responsibility will be to educate yourself and your child about the most prevalent forms of mental health issues: depression, bipolar disorder, anxiety, and post-traumatic stress disorder. It will also be important that you strive to shatter myths about such experiences being an unavoidable, unchangeable aspect of Asperger's Syndrome and to keep an open communication going with your child so she knows she can approach you with any issues that may develop.

Prevention, Not Intervention

Mental health is one of the driving factors in "behaviors." It is also the most ambiguous factor. Psychiatry, the practice of diagnosing probable mental health conditions, is not an exact science. Determining a mental health diagnosis is predicated upon educated attempts to pin down the intangible. There is no single psychiatrist who can unequivocally state the precise mental health experience of any given individual; the experience is unique to each individual, so it may manifest in many nuances. The best a doctor can do is make an educated best guess based upon his professional expertise. He does this in conjunction with observing and interviewing a client and consulting the *DSM* (or other clinical documents) to narrow it down to a diagnosis based upon a series of symptoms—what the client reports of her experiences and how she presents during the interview.

There is a long-standing stereotype that perpetuates the belief that "junk behaviors" in people with different ways of being (including Asperger's Syndrome) are merely byproducts of those experiences. But knowledge is power and, as a conscious parent, your approach should be one of prevention instead of intervention. Remember the self-fulfilling prophecy? Understanding how to successfully avert its vicious cycle will directly influence your child's mental health.

To begin with, it is important to outwardly express your love and caring for your child in ways that she understands, using concrete pictures, words, and actions paired with validating statements. For example, you could set aside times to spend with your child and sing her favorite songs or create an arts and crafts project that builds upon one of her most passionate interests, while acknowledging that you love her and love sharing this kind of time with her. Together you are creating life movies for future replay.

Reinforce to your child that your love is unconditional—a tough concept for many kids, let alone the child with Asperger's, to grasp. Explain to your child that, even though she may make mistakes or do things you disapprove of, your love is constant and will never waver. Be certain to praise her accomplishments, gifts, and talents often. Highlight her successes, and tell her how happy and proud she makes you feel. Tell others about the amazing things she's accomplished as well, and, with her prior okay, make such comments publicly in her presence. Ask her to show you exactly how she did what she did and tell her how much you've enjoyed listening to her (even if she gets long-winded). Tell your child with Asperger's Syndrome that she is beautiful—not just physically beautiful, but truly beautiful inside. Tell her that her inner beauty is that of being a good human being who wants to give of her gifts and talents to others. Discuss how this inner beauty is the most valuable of all, far more important than physical attractiveness.

Why all the emphasis on glorifying your child? In doing so, you are incrementally fortifying the child with Asperger's Syndrome by laying a foundation of strong self-esteem. This will serve as ammunition as your child grows and enters adolescence and beyond. Never underestimate the power and long-lasting effect of your most loving words and actions. Your child will retain and replay the most memorable of such experiences for the rest of her life. They will buoy her when she needs it most.

Depression

The mental health experience of depression is extremely common in people with Asperger's Syndrome. Many otherwise brilliant and gifted adults are significantly derailed or crippled by its effects. They are stymied and unable to move forward, as their Asperger's experience is compounded by the symptoms of depression.

More than ever, it has become imperative that you, as a conscious parent, be aware and attentive to changes in your child's mood and overall affect. We live in an era in which mass shootings in public places or schools have seemingly become a monthly occurrence. In several instances, the perpetrators were young men considered to be loners or social outcasts, leading the media to speculate that these individuals had Asperger's. This may or may not have been the case, but the speculation has had a tremendously negative effect on people's perceptions of "weird" kids who are bullied and who self-isolate from their peer groups. It is important to engage with your child about any troubling issues while demystifying his incorrect perception by others.

Parents should be mindful of the potential for depression in children with Asperger's starting from about age ten on (although, in some instances, environment and genetic predisposition can induce depression earlier). This is the age when, more than ever, typical children are propelled into preadolescence with lightning speed. They may:

○ Begin to define their personal individuality based upon older role models

○ Give more attention to personal appearance, style, and taste

○ Take on more mature interests typical of preteens

○ Pair up and develop cliques or specific circles of friends designated by certain criteria (athletic aptitude, superior physical appearance, or academic achievement)

○ Become more aware of differences in others

This is the time when, more than ever, the child with Asperger's who doesn't feel included may become more aware of her own differences or be made to feel different by others. When this occurs consistently and she is without a solid, loving foundation from which to draw strength, she becomes especially vulnerable to depression.

WHAT CAUSES DEPRESSION?

Like most mental health problems, depression is linked to a chemical imbalance in the brain. It may develop as a result of family genetics (a history of mental health issues on either side of one's lineage) or environmental factors, such as the child who falls victim to poor self-esteem through some form of abuse. It may be triggered by an event (or series of events) that so changes the way one is accustomed to being in the world that recovery and return to normalcy is difficult. And depression may be brought on by a chronic, deteriorating physical condition.

If you sense that depression may be a possibility for your child, it will be important to become savvy about its symptoms and how it may manifest through your child's words and actions. It will be equally important, especially at this time, to recall the positive philosophies as they apply to your child. And remember, mental health problems, including depression, are no one's fault.

> Chronic endurance of physical pain and discomfort without adequate relief can induce depression. Think of those you've known grappling with cancer or some other intense, long-term physical ailment. It is easy for anyone to succumb to depression under such devastating circumstances.

Depression is defined using a list of symptoms. As an aid, those general symptoms are indicated here as they may appear in any child, but they are embellished with specifics to show how depression may appear differently in the child with Asperger's. When examining the signs of depression or other mental health problems, it is very important to bear in mind that the symptoms:

O Must be significant differences from what is typical demeanor for your child

O Must occur in clusters or groups—single symptoms in isolation do not a syndrome make

Additionally, pay attention to the presence of any "cycles," that is, times of year during which your child experiences differences in how she talks and acts. Such cycles could correlate with "off schedule" changes in routine such as holidays and school in-service days or vacations. Cycles could also match up with sad anniversary dates or even seasonal changes. Genetics and family history can also affect your child's experience. This includes not only mental health history but also alcoholism or substance abuse in families. People in denial or who believe that accessing mental health services is stigmatizing will often self-medicate using these substances.

WHAT ARE THE SYMPTOMS?

The foremost symptom of depression is that of an overall depressed mood. This includes spontaneous crying and weeping (for no reason apparent to you), whining, moaning, or a general sense of sadness and melancholy longer than two weeks in duration. This type of behavior would not be considered a symptom if it followed a death or significant life-changing event (such as the family moving and changing schools), after which it would be typical for your child to mourn.

Remember to be sensitive about how your child processes a loss. The child with Asperger's cannot simply "get over it" in reaction to a situation that others may consider insignificant. Be mindful that your child may grieve over losses that are not readily perceptible by you.

Abuse by peers can contribute to depression and even post-traumatic stress disorder. Additionally, if your child is severely depressed, she may feel such worthlessness that she deliberately antagonizes bullies or instigates further abuse by "offering" herself up to them, being well aware of the impending harm.

A depressed child may seem fascinated by morbid thoughts about funerals, disease, and death. The preteen or adolescent may despair, not wanting to be seen as "different." Your child may make remarks that are self-deprecating such as "No one loves me," "I hate myself," "What's the use," or "I'm not wanted here." In extreme instances, your child may try to seriously harm herself by attempting suicide or recklessly placing herself in harm's way.

Another symptom of depression is a decreased interest in pleasurable activities. If your child is depressed, this symptom will likely be quite distinct because she has lost all or most desire for her most passionate area of interest. Your child may pass up opportunities to participate in activities related to her passion or intentionally withdraw from those activities in favor of isolation or seclusion from others. (This includes intentionally setting herself up to be forcibly excluded or grounded via parental discipline.) Your child may also give away or destroy items that you immediately recognize as personally valuable or meaningful to her.

Additional, supporting symptoms of depression may include:

O Increased agitation

O Psychomotor retardation, which is an overall, noticeable "slowing down"

O Fatigue and difficulty in physical movement (in which the smallest of feats requires great effort)

O Clinginess, meaning that your child wants to physically "hang" on you and needs repeated assurances that everything is okay

O Requiring too much or too little sleep or being difficult to rouse

O Loss of appetite or feeling nauseated at the sight of food (or your child may try to make herself feel better by eating too much food—especially sugary or fatty snack foods)

O Seeming confused, listless, or disoriented (or your child may urinate in places other than the toilet, such as a corner of her room or, if a boy, in a dresser drawer)

Again, some or all of these symptoms may manifest in any child but may appear more peculiar or intense in the child with Asperger's.

Bipolar Disorder

You've just reviewed some symptoms that may be indicators of depression. Many people find themselves depressed at various points in their lives; it is a fairly natural thing. Depression is a mental health problem that can "stand alone." This means it can occur without association with another mental health problem.

When someone has a bipolar mental health experience, there are two components to it. Depression is one of those two components. The other is called mania. While depression can occur without mania, mania never stands alone without depression at some point.

The characters from the classic *Winnie-the-Pooh* stories make a good bipolar analogy. Think about Tigger the tiger and Eeyore the donkey. Tigger demonstrates the intense, "wired" energy and grandiose self-esteem associated with mania. Eeyore is typically self-loathing, lethargic, and full of hopelessness for the future. If their personalities were combined in a single character, that character would be the epitome of bipolar disorder.

You may have heard people described using the outdated label "manic-depressive"; this term refers to someone who experiences bipolar disorder. (Bipolar means two opposite ends of the poles, or two extremes—mania and depression.) Bipolar may also be referred to as severe "mood swings." When someone has bipolar disorder, there may be periods when she is level or even. She may experience the onset of a manic experience that may develop gradually or skyrocket rapidly—it all depends on the individual. At some point, the person de-escalates from mania and either returns to feeling level or begins a descent into depression. Many people feel similar highs and dips, but these usually do not impair their daily lives. The difference here is that being bipolar can seriously affect one's life if not properly treated. In fact, a 2008 study by researchers in the Department of Neuropsychiatry at Kanazawa University Hospital, Kanazawa, Japan, concluded that of the forty-four adolescents and young adults with Asperger's examined, the major co-occurring mental health issue identified was bipolar disorder. The study also suggested that Asperger's and bipolar may share common genes. If accurate, this is all the more reason to be diligent in ascertaining your child's mental wellness.

You are now familiar with the primary symptoms of depression as they may appear in your child. Now review the symptoms of mania for any child, augmented with details specific to a different way of being.

MOOD SWINGS

The first major symptom of mania is a euphoric or irritable mood. Your child may seem delirious or giddy, with an increased intensity of laughing and grinning. At times she may have a fixed grin and speech that appears forced or unnatural. Her speech may be pressured, meaning it is bursting forth hard and fast as though her thoughts are speeding. You may notice your child forcing laughter at inappropriate times, such as during serious discussions. If your child has always been a "kidder," you may notice her taking things too far, unable to cease the joke-telling or pushing physical slapstick that gets out of hand or causes others harm. Your child's tolerance threshold for autistic-like sensory sensitivities may also be vastly diminished, heightening irritability.

INFLATED SELF-ESTEEM

The next manic symptom is a sense of inflated self-esteem, known as grandiosity. A child with Asperger's may project a sense of omnipotence and control over those in authority such as Mom, Dad, teachers, doctors, or caregivers. She may "hire" or "fire" you, threaten to withhold your salary, or physically direct you and others where to go in a given environment. In one instance, a young boy insisted, "God's not the boss, I am!"

The child may believe him- or herself to be a childhood "celebrity" such as a popular TV, movie, or cartoon character, or even Santa Claus. The child may try to assume all or part of an authority figure's name. Similarly, the child may believe she possesses superhuman "superhero" strength. She may climb on top of furniture, windowsills, and countertops, out onto rooftops, or into the street. There, she may hurl herself into space with the belief that she will fly, or that no harm will come to her. Grandiosity may also manifest in your child damaging property, like trashing her bedroom or attempting to lift and throw heavy objects such as a television or pieces of furniture.

In extreme instances, your child may smear or throw feces, or urinate in places other than the bathroom. You may notice your child hoarding food or taking someone else's food, even if she has the same portions in front of her. Finally, and most significantly, your child may physically attack and harm people very dear to her—people she would otherwise never dream of hurting. This may include hitting, punching, pulling hair, biting, scratching, head-butting, pinching, or using weapons like knives. Once the manic "high" has blown over, it is very common for many children with Asperger's to be extremely remorseful for their actions during the times they were not in control. They may sob bitterly, want to be held, or plead for forgiveness.

OBSESSIONS

Another primary symptom of mania is an increased intensity in pleasurable activities. This is when the child's special areas of interest, or passions, may seem like obsessions. The child's focus may be so absorbed that she cannot be dissuaded away from the activity. If you insist, she may lash out verbally or physically. For some children, especially teens, this symptom may come through with a sexual intensity, called hypersexuality. He or she may make wildly inappropriate remarks to others (including adults), touch others without permission, or masturbate openly or with greater frequency.

OTHER SYMPTOMS OF MANIA

Instead of jumping to conclusions about "delinquent behavior," see if other symptoms support a case for mania. Additional symptoms of mania may include:

O Increased agitation, as though your child has a "short fuse"

O Being "wired" with energy (perhaps she doesn't sleep, sometimes for days in a row, or naps sporadically)

O Having changes in appetite (such as gorging herself or hoarding food, possibly in dresser drawers or under her bed)

O Having "racing" thoughts or ideas (for example, rapidly shifts topics without any apparent connection between them; seems physically indecisive, moving from one activity to another without any rationale; talks at a very fast pace, tripping over words or spitting while talking)

If your child is bipolar and she experiences periods of mania and depression, it will be important to stay focused on the child, not the behaviors. This will be your single greatest challenge as a parent. Remember, it is not your child's fault. It is no one's fault, but it is serious, and you must be aggressive in seeking relief for your child through proper treatment.

Anxiety and Post-Traumatic Stress Disorder

Mood disorders (depression or bipolar disorder) are commonplace mental health experiences for the general population, and especially for people with different ways of being, including those with Asperger's Syndrome. Because of the pervasiveness of mood disorders, the *DSM* compels a clinician to rule them out first. Afterward, other mental health problems, including those that may occur concurrently with a mood disorder, may be considered.

ANXIETY

When most people think about kids with Asperger's and mental health issues, they often think about anxiety. Anxiety is typical of many children with Asperger's because of their gentle and sensitive nature and their need to feel safe and comfortable within a range of predictability. Everybody feels nervous or anxious about certain things in their lives, and as a parent, you know that the things you consider minor can snowball into something huge for your child. "Big world" complexities may seem beyond your child's control, and her perceptions can become exaggerated or blown out of proportion. Some kids really torture themselves, agonizing over details, particularly with regard to the future. Events such as impending appointments, tests, or social activities—especially those in which your child is expected to "perform" or excel—can cause her to be unable to keep things in perspective or keep anxiety in check. Your child's anxiety may also be driven by feelings of distress or guilt due to family disharmony.

You may notice your child's anxiety through her inability to remain calm, focused, and rested. She may ruminate on certain topics or request that you confirm the same information over and over again.

Your ability to be better attuned to your own thoughts and feelings as a mindful parent will enable you to set an example of open and honest communication with your child. Encourage your child early on to communicate her concerns to you, no matter how minor. Some kids are martyrs, believing they must suffer in silence; so if your child approaches you with a complaint, accept it as legitimate to her. Process the day with your child at bedtime and provide soothing assurances or a plan to make things right as part of a nightly ritual.

So what can a parent do to help an anxious child? You may very well be doing your anxious child a disservice by not trying to first understand the roots of her anxiety or provide coping strategies to help her independently relieve stress and anxiety.

POST-TRAUMATIC STRESS DISORDER

In many instances, anxieties can escalate into post-traumatic stress disorder (PTSD) if they are not addressed. This is especially true if your child has participated in or been the target of abuse (in any form) or has witnessed some disturbing or violent event, such as a car accident.

The symptoms of PTSD may look very similar to depression, but remember that, per the *DSM* guidelines, depression must be explored first. Additional symptoms of PTSD may include:

O Having nightmares and night sweats

O Re-enacting sexual abuse or attempting to impose sexual behavior upon others

O Showing clinginess or a general sense of fearfulness

- Increasingly withdrawing from social activities

- Having flashbacks, triggered by people, places, visuals, and smells (your child may replay mind movies at this time)

- Acting out past events verbally, physically, or both

- Bedwetting

- Feeling unsafe or unprotected in familiar environments, or violently refusing to be in a particular environment

- Complaining of feeling physically or sexually "dirty," and desiring to bathe frequently

- Illustrating a traumatic experience through writing, art, or music

- Being hypervigilant, which means appearing to be "on guard" or being easily startled

It is imperative that you support your child to the best of your ability to work toward resolving issues of depression, bipolar disorder, anxiety, and PTSD. The future of her mental health and her capacity to function as an effective contributor to her community depend upon it.

Approaches for Mental Health Care

It is often difficult for parents to see the forest for the trees. That is, people tend to recall major, cataclysmic behavioral "events," as opposed to being objective and stepping back to notice a trend or cycle of symptoms. Some parents may also struggle with issues of guilt or denial. This is where consulting with a professional will be of great value.

FINDING A PSYCHIATRIST

The challenge may be finding a clinician who is abreast of recent "best practice" trends (what is presently acknowledged as the "right," or respectful, approach) and does not buy into stereotypes that your child's behavior results from being a kid with Asperger's. As with seeking the initial diagnosis for Asperger's or ASD, you may encounter difficulty in locating a psychiatrist who meets this criterion. This is where networking with other parents or ASD organizations in your area may be helpful. As before, be prepared to travel, especially if you live in a rural area and resources are sparse.

There's a phrase used to describe untreated mental health issues: "The longer the needle plays on the record, the deeper the groove becomes." If your child demonstrates highly unusual or out-of-control behaviors, please actively seek timely clinical support.

PREPARING FOR THE FIRST VISIT

If you believe that your child is experiencing a mental health issue, prepare yourself and your child for the appointment with the psychiatrist just as you would for the appointment to interview for a diagnosis (review these steps in Chapter 3). In addition, it will be of greatest benefit to a psychiatrist if you come prepared to discuss symptoms and not behaviors. This text has provided you with the language used to describe symptoms—euphoric mood, grandiosity, and the like. This is language a good doctor will recognize and understand.

You know your child best; a psychiatrist is especially vulnerable to whatever you do and say. After all, unless you have a previously established rapport, he's meeting you and your child for the first time. You have an obligation to your child to be direct and concise and to stay focused on discussing symptoms. When you enter a doctor's office venting with lots of storytelling about how difficult it was last weekend when your child trashed the house, punched her sister, and threw a TV out a second-story window, you are discussing behaviors. It may be natural to want to do this, especially with someone who you hope will understand, validate your experience, and provide you with answers. However, in describing behaviors, you've just significantly broadened the doctor's challenge; the previously listed "behaviors" can correspond to dozens of potential diagnoses. When this occurs, you risk your doctor "falling back" on ascribing stereotyped diagnoses like schizophrenia, borderline personality disorder, obsessive-compulsive disorder, oppositional defiant disorder, or intermittent explosive disorder.

You can prepare for an initial appointment with a psychiatrist by doing the following:

○ Organize your child's symptoms as best you can by breaking them into categories for depression or bipolar to start.

○ After listing out the previous two, list symptoms of anxiety and PTSD.

○ Keep everything brief and concise—to one page if possible. Use numbered or bulleted entries so your doctor can easily scan the information.

○ Be prepared to discuss your family's mental health history (including alcohol and substance abuse) and any cycles you have noted in your child.

○ Do not provide the doctor with anything more than what he is requesting, but be prepared to offer it if he does. This could include information about your child's previous physical ailments and operations or traumatic experiences such as the loss of a loved one or a tragic accident.

○ Become educated about medications traditionally used to treat mood disorders, such as lithium, Depakote, and Tegretol, and other newer mood stabilizers such as Lamictal, Zyprexa, Trileptal, Neurontin, and Topamax. (Be wary of antipsychotic medications except for short-term use in extreme, out-of-control instances.)

○ Ensure either that your child will participate in a gentle, respectful discussion with the doctor or that there is someone with whom your child can stay in a waiting area while you discuss specifics that may be very upsetting for your child to hear.

CONSIDERING SHORT-TERM HOSPITALIZATION

If your child's symptoms manifest in extreme, violent behavior that causes her to seriously endanger herself or others, you may also need to carefully weigh the option of a short-term commitment to a psychiatric hospital in order to keep her and your family safe. The goal of a short-term hospitalization is to stabilize the child as soon and as safely as possible prior to discharge back to her family. There, she can receive observation and treatment in a controlled environment. The treatment may include medication to stabilize her and help her to feel level again.

In gaining control over violent behavior, antipsychotic medications will likely be prescribed. Such medications are usually strong sedatives, intended to "slow down" the child so that she will be manageable and less of a threat to herself and others. Such antipsychotic medications may include Thorazine (chlorpromazine), Mellaril (thioridazine), Serentil (mesoridazine), Prolixin (fluphenazine), Stelazine (trifluoperazine), Haldol (haloperidol), and Loxitane (loxapine). It is not usual for such powerful drugs to be used to treat children, and their sedative effect in your child may be alarming. Be mindful that such drugs should be temporary until the mood-stabilizing medications take effect. Your role as a strong advocate for your child is to be educated about the names of medications, the reason for their prescription, their duration and desired effects, and any adverse side effects. This is not a time to be shy or self-conscious, or to feel inferior—don't be afraid to ask and re-ask important questions or to request a second opinion if you are feeling dissatisfied. If you suspect your child is experiencing mental health issues, it is imperative that you take proactive action to address them before the situation escalates into a severe crisis.

Fostering Mental Health Self-Advocacy

Many people with Asperger's—adults and children—grapple with anxiety, depression, and other mental health issues. Psychiatric diagnosis and medication may become a way of life, especially if the individual receives clinical benefit from this approach. The caveat lies in parents believing that this is the sole answer. Remember, the key is prevention, not intervention. It's never too early to shower your child with adoration and accolades that will become a foundation of strength for her. Finding a medication regime that is a good match is a trial-and-error process that may take time, sometimes months or years.

Teaching your child mindfulness is a great technique for practicing prevention, not intervention. When your child is able to slow down, focus on breathing, and center herself, she decreases her anxiety, is less emotionally reactive, is more self-accepting, and is more able to handle daily challenges. The emotional regulation that comes from mindfulness—the ability to quiet one's mind—helps your child un-identify with her negative thoughts and realize that they are not who she is. These prove to be invaluable skills for your child to develop.

Instilling mindfulness in your child can also come from creating an informal circle of support around her that also includes her. This will provide her with an unconditional place of communion with those who know and care for her best. The circle should create a positive, personalized plan of support—a map or blueprint—to complement the Individualized Education Program (IEP), psychiatric treatment plan, or other types of written documents designed to assist your child.

If you have confirmed that your child is grappling with a mental health problem, empower her to become self-aware in order to grow into a strong self-advocate. Her ability to recognize her symptoms and know her needs is of great importance.

Another strategy that has been effective is to partner with the child to draw the mental health problem as she envisions it. What has worked with many children is to have them imagine a car in which they are competing for control of the driver's seat. In the driver's seat, you're in control of the car, but if your mental health problem takes control, you may be bumped to the passenger seat, with limited control—or worse yet, you're bumped to the backseat or the trunk. Many children are able to accurately tell, on any given day, exactly where they are positioned in the car. The ability to independently articulate her mental health experience will be of lifelong value for your child.

Important Points to Consider

The best help you can give your child in terms of mental health is to educate her and yourself. Know that while some mental disorders do frequently occur with Asperger's, they are not certainties. And if your child does begin to exhibit some symptoms of other mental health conditions, be there to support and help her in any way you can. Education is the best prevention. Some additional points to consider are:

O Educate yourself and your child's doctor on your family medical history.

O Know the signs and symptoms of the mental illnesses in this chapter so you can intervene immediately if your child begins to display them.

O Be patient and loving with your child, and shower her with praise and accolades that can help bolster her mental state during difficult times.

O Help your child be her own advocate. If she can clearly understand her condition, she can seek out help when she needs it.

 **CHAPTER 7**

Passions

Your child with Asperger's may have intense interest in one or more specific areas, such as types of insects, the names of racehorses, movies about space, or how engines work. As a conscious parent, you should try to become involved in your child's passions. Showing that you "get" the importance of his areas of interest lets him know that he is valued and has much to offer others. And as your child grows, these particular areas of interest can be used as links to life-defining opportunities in learning, relationships, and employment.

Identifying and Valuing Personal Passions

Many children with Asperger's have an absolute fascination with certain subject or topic areas and quickly become encyclopedic in their knowledge. Others may classify this fascination as an "obsession," but what's wrong with a child who loves learning so much that he takes any opportunity to add to his knowledge? After all, the world's most advanced thinkers, talented artists, and brilliant inventors propelled whole cultures with their astounding expertise.

Be an advocate for your child and his passions. Recognize the remarkable amount of information he is able to retain. Sharing in a passion may be the best way for you and your child to connect on a daily basis.

Your child may be passionate about a school subject that he excels in, such as mathematics, physics, or music. He may also indulge his passion through extracurricular classes or clubs, or after-school or weekend activities.

He may "set you up" by asking you questions that have answers only he knows, and then feign disbelief that you don't provide the very complex, intricate, correct response. If you've been through this drill before, your child may even become perturbed that, by now, you haven't memorized the appropriate answer in order to "play along." It's easy to become annoyed or distracted by your child's focus or to feel that it represents "abnormal" behavior. But if you stop and take the time to listen to him, you might be surprised to find that talking about a passion is a great way to connect with your child.

Here are some things that your child may be passionate about:

- Wheels or other parts of automobiles, trains, trucks, tractors, and planes

- Oceanography and marine life species

- Astronomy, planets, and constellations

- Cartoon animation and comics

- Music, especially classical music

- The animal kingdom, including specific creatures such as horses, reptiles, or insects

- Architecture

- The human body and how it works

- Dinosaurs

- Specific movies or movie series such as *The Wizard of Oz, Star Wars,* or *Star Trek*

- Famous people such as prominent scientists and researchers, actors and comedians, religious figures, or U.S. presidents

This list is by no means all-inclusive; the variety of potential passions is endless. You may find your child steeped in his passion at every opportunity—it's what he wants as gifts for birthdays and holidays or what he enjoys talking about with visiting relatives. You may be astounded at the depth of detail with which your child can conjure up information at will and without effort. He could spend hours absorbed in his most passionate interests, to the point where you might have to insist he take periodic breaks.

Be mindful that your child's seemingly endless outpouring of "stuff" related to his passion(s) is his way of communicating something meaningful to you. One divorced dad keeps current with his son's interest in heavy metal bands so that the time they share is made that much more memorable for both because of the in-depth conversations they have.

Above all else, though, understand that your child's personality is defined by his passions; the two are that closely aligned. How you receive and accept your child's passions will directly affect the quality of your parent-child relationship. You may demonstrate that you value your child's passion by:

- Acknowledging it as a good thing

- Realizing that it is a form of communication

- Acknowledging its importance to your child

- Making time to interact with your child (looking and listening) about his passion

- Asking probing questions so that you may learn more

- Asking questions designed to get your child thinking and imagining possibilities related to his passion

- Suggesting ways your child may introduce family and friends to his passion

- Partnering with your child to research facets of his passion

- Participating in out-of-house opportunities you or your child arrange that involve his passion

One mom historically dismissed her son's "ramblings" about the nuances of building construction until she decided to ask him questions about his current topic of discussion (concrete versus cement—who knew there was a distinction?) and, for the first time ever, they enjoyed a ten-minute dialogue they otherwise never would have had. At the conclusion of her tutorial, her son exuberantly asked his mom for a hug, and a new beginning occurred for their parent-child relationship. Now that's a reward!

Passions and Relationship Building

In addition to strengthening his personal relationship with you, your child's passions can be used to develop additional relationships with others. Because he can discuss his passions endlessly, it will be important to try to connect him with others similarly impassioned. Your child may already understand that he cannot talk about his passions at school during classroom instruction. But there are other outlets that the school day can provide for social opportunities that build upon his passions. Such opportunities will require the cooperation of teachers, teachers' aides, and others to set up a structure within which the social interactions may occur.

CREATING A COMFORTABLE ENVIRONMENT

The lunchroom is often challenging and overwhelming for many children with Asperger's Syndrome. It is usually a large, open area filled with many, many children all talking at once. Sometimes there is music playing, silverware clanking, and a social protocol involving where and with whom one sits.

Creating "lunch bunch" tables may be an appealing alternative for any number of kids. Your child may know of other children with similar passions, or his teachers may be able to help identify them, even if they are in other grades. Talk to your child's teacher about the possibility of setting up an area of lunch bunch tables in the cafeteria. The concept is to establish a welcoming structure and routine by assigning students to tables and lunchtime discussion topics based upon their mutual (or similar) passions. If possible, the tables could be moved off to one side of the cafeteria, away from the distracting noise and visuals, to help foster successful conversations.

To start, an adult may help to regulate the conversation, moving the conversation through lulls, and modeling acceptable turn-taking. These discussions provide structure during a typically unstructured time (during which some kids with Asperger's socially flounder). It is nonstigmatizing because the opportunity to participate is open to all, and, depending upon assigned topics, may even come to be seen as "cool."

Other opportunities to connect socially while building upon passions include after-school clubs, the library, camps, scouts, and other extracurricular activities such as art lessons, horseback riding, martial arts, or swimming.

COMMUNICATING VIA THE INTERNET

An interaction doesn't have to be in person to be "social." How many people do you know in your life whom you rarely see but stay in touch with by phone, texting, or e-mail? Interacting with others using the computer is social! There are countless opportunities to make social contacts with others through topic-specific websites, chat rooms, message boards, e-mail, and instant messaging. It's important to explain to your child the rules, cautions, and expectations of using the Internet, including a list of topics that are not appropriate for discussion. You may also wish to counsel your child on the pros and cons of whether to sign up for popular social media sites, especially if she is easily manipulated by peers or vulnerable to becoming a target of an online bullying campaign.

You may be quite surprised by the eloquent and articulate manner in which some people with Asperger's or ASD communicate by e-mail—folks who might otherwise seem socially awkward during in-person dialogue. The reasons for their success include:

- No pressure to respond verbally

- No pressure to reply with immediacy, as in real-time conversation

- No pressure to make eye contact

- No external stimuli or visual distraction to detract focus

- The luxury of taking time to think and answer thoughtfully

- The opportunity to edit communication before sending a message

- No fear of being judged by others based on appearance

- The pleasure of interacting with others with the same passions

If you or your child is computer savvy, you may even create a personal web page, blog, or website to connect people through mutual passions. A circle of friends may grow to international proportions. Additionally, if your child is interested, he should be encouraged to exchange e-mail addresses with friendly classmates in order to maintain social connections after school, on weekends, over long holidays, and especially during summer vacation. Kids who don't do well conversing by phone because they monopolize the conversation—or have very chatty peers who monopolize the conversation—really flourish when using e-mail to discuss common interests and passions. In fact, you may even glean information from your child that he might not offer orally, in person, by sending him an e-mail.

CHALLENGES

One challenge your child may face in sharing his passion with his same-age peers, particularly as he enters his teen years, is if the passion is considered juvenile or "babyish." For example, consider the teenage boy who loves the *Powerpuff Girls* cartoon series. His passion is genuine, and yet he should exercise discretion to avoid being set up as a target of ridicule because of the way others may perceive it. This is a common issue for many children with Asperger's who have passions that have been long-standing since childhood. Such passions may remain constant while the interests of his peers mature into more dynamic areas typical of teens.

> Part of conscious parenting means thinking outside the box and approaching circumstances from a different perspective. It's becoming easier for the person with Asperger's Syndrome to justify indulging in his passions because nowadays many people are avid collectors of memorabilia devoted to their hobbies. This is an authentic and legitimate manner to reinterpret your child's special interests.

The strategy here is twofold. First, privately, gently, and respectfully counsel your child about the ways in which his passion may be perceived. Let him know that you "get" it and value it, but explain that others may not see it that way. List the people who can be trusted to discuss the passion unconditionally and without judgment. Next, list places in which it is okay to discuss the passion with these people with some modicum of privacy so others will not overhear, such as your own or a friend's house.

Second, coach your child to practice "upgrading" the manner in which he presents his passion to others. This means putting a sophisticated spin on it, such as emphasizing how the *Powerpuff Girls* animation team creates the cartoons, or discussing a recent Internet auction in which a rare, limited-edition, foreign-market "Bubbles" figurine brought an amazing bid. Articulating this knowledge will go over better than discussing the nuances of a particular episode.

Passions As Bridges to Learning

Children with Asperger's Syndrome have an amazing capacity to learn, but they may struggle in areas that they're not passionate about. But you and your child's teachers have the opportunity to tie his passions to other subjects. For example, if he is immersed in the world of horses, encourage him to learn about how their anatomy works, how to calculate how fast they run, and even what the complicated names of racehorses mean. If he enjoys plants, talk to him about Latin roots in the names of plants, how to lay out a garden for maximum output, or what a leaf looks like under a microscope.

Schedule a pre-IEP (Individualized Education Program) meeting to discuss with your child's teachers the subjects with which he is struggling. Come prepared to share your child's passions (with his permission or, better yet, his involvement) and brainstorm ways you can all help him to deconstruct areas of learning using his passions as analogies to understanding.

Trieste is a mindful mom who understands the value of her son's passion for numbers coupled with putting him in control of his passion.

From age one, my son's passions were letters and numbers. He was reading at eighteen months, and he could count to 500—backward and forward, by odds and evens—by age two. We used both these passions as tools to help him learn numerous skills. Since he loved to read, we presented him with as much information as possible in both written and verbal forms. One example: As a preschooler, he had difficulty following verbal directions from his occupational therapist who wanted him to complete an "obstacle course" of various motor tasks. We placed a large chalkboard in the room and on it we wrote and numbered each of the steps of the obstacle course. He was delighted to read each step aloud and followed the directions easily once he saw them in writing.

When it came to numbers, his object of desire was (and still is!) a digital runner's watch. We carried that watch with us everywhere. One experience I vividly recall is teaching my son to tolerate haircuts. I found a shop that specialized in children's haircuts and zeroed in on a stylist who was particularly patient and easygoing. With the stylist's cooperation, my son would set his stopwatch for five seconds while the stylist cut five "snips" of hair. We increased the time to ten seconds and ten snips, twenty seconds and twenty snips, and so on until, after many, many months, my son could tolerate a complete haircut without any breaks. Although getting a haircut was uncomfortable for my son, he loved the fact that the grownups were sharing in his "watch passion." The look of pure joy on his face when adults played "watch games" with him gave me an early lesson in the value of using passions as bridges to learning and to building relationships.

Never underestimate the power of your child's passions. Think about your child's most passionate interests and brainstorm with him, as well as family and friends, to come up with ways to use the passion to deconstruct and make clearer those areas most challenging to learn. Once you get the hang of it, it will be an enjoyable and bonding experience for all.

Passions As Bridges to Employment

The subject areas your child is passionate about directly relate to his way of being in the world and his aptitude for branching out to learn new things, especially things that may be challenging to grasp. It makes sense to foster your child's areas of specialty to their fullest potential to prepare him for future employment opportunities. Many adults work at jobs they dislike, but the luckiest have jobs that they love because the jobs interest them.

The time to encourage your child to learn and consume all he can about his passions is now! It doesn't matter that he is a child; he still has the opportunity to become the foremost expert in his field, and that can lead to satisfying employment opportunities.

Foster your child's passions while he is in elementary and middle school, and the range of employment will be far greater when his specialty niche has been so clearly defined, and his role in life is apparent to all.

Bonnie's son, Noel, is ten. He has a passion for the gaming system GameCube. His fascination with all the games' characters enables him to understand what they do and how they do it. Learning the details and game-specific terminology is like learning another language. Bonnie is supporting Noel in developing career goals based upon his passion. For example, Noel wants to develop GameCube games using 3ds Max and Flash. He also dreams of developing medical applications using robotics. Bonnie adds:

> Noel wants to learn more about space with the idea that he can use knowledge about gravityless environments to do his inventions or to do space travel (he figures he can use his quick eye-hand coordination that he's developed from playing GameCube). The goals may seem far-reaching or unachievable, but it's not our job as parents to judge this. My job is to help him make the connection between his interests and how he can use that.

The positive approach Bonnie is taking with Noel by building on his passions will be invaluable to him as he grows and furthers his education in pursuit of his visions.

When Is a Passion a Problem?

If your child's desire for his passion becomes all-consuming and unusually intense, it may be cause for concern. Obsessive-compulsive disorder (OCD) occurs when your child has thoughts (obsessions) or physical actions (compulsions) that seem out of his control, and they become unpleasant, very stressful, or harmful for him. This may or may not involve his passion; it may involve some new, seemingly odd or purposeless focus on a bodily function, for example, or the need to repeatedly check his hands for cleanliness. Some "red flag" indicators that your child may have OCD could include the following:

O He is quick to lash out and becomes verbally or physically abusive when you try to redirect him away from his activity.

O His need to indulge in his activity causes him to lose sleep, skip meals, or be late for school.

O He withdraws from family, friends, and pets in favor of spending unusual amounts of time involved in the activity.

O He cannot seem to focus on or discuss anything but the activity.

O He has lost interest in his appearance, dress, and hygiene because the activity has become all-consuming.

If you note any of these changes in your child, it will be important for you to gather information about what you are observing in order to prepare for meeting with a psychiatrist. Follow the same protocol of preparation for such an appointment as you would when seeking an initial diagnosis or exploring other mental health issues.

If your child takes medication, it is important that he is a partner in understanding why and knowing its potential side effects. One young boy with Asperger's quite clearly communicated how his OCD medication made him feel, saying, "It makes me crazy"—and this showed in his behavior. Listen to your child and consult with your doctor to appropriately adjust or discontinue medication that is not a good match for your child.

In the interim, if your child's passions fit the OCD criteria, you may find yourself needing to reinforce parental parameters by being very firm about scheduling activities and responsibilities and holding your child accountable. Use visual time frames such as calendars, clocks, and watches, and personal schedules to set limits for the amount of time your child is permitted to indulge in an activity, if you can abide it as socially acceptable. Educators will also need to be clear and concrete about rules and responsibilities during the school day. Apply proper disciplinary measures once you ensure that all expectations have been made clear to your child.

Appropriate medication may be a sound, time-limited resource for your child, but medication can do only so much. If your child receives a clinical OCD diagnosis it will be important to reflect upon the whole person—what's going on in his life and what might be driving this experience? Possible causes or triggers that might exacerbate a predisposition to OCD could include peer pressure and bullying, academic challenges, concerns about future life-changing events, or overwhelming adjustments in personal relationships, to name a few. Remember that this is a mental health experience that is not your child's fault and may well be beyond his immediate control.

Important Points to Consider

If your child is passionate about something, embrace it. Showing interest in your child's passion opens up the opportunity for communicating and bonding with him, and those are always positive things. Here are some points to keep in mind about your child's passions:

- ○ Your child's passion is of the utmost importance to him. Try to respect his passion and never belittle it.

- ○ Strengthen your knowledge about your child's passion so you can discuss and share things about it. You will be surprised at how much your child appreciates this.

- ○ Allow avenues for your child to explore his passion. Even if his passion is far-fetched in your eyes, find ways that he can explore it as much as possible.

- ○ Find creative ways for your child to use his passion to overcome obstacles or other areas he is uncomfortable in.

- ○ Help your child expand his social circle through exploring his passion with like-minded people or groups.

 **CHAPTER 8**

Family Dynamics

Though your communication with your children may be as respectful and fair as it can be, there are times when family dynamics can be challenging and complex. This is especially true when you are faced with learning how best to support a child newly diagnosed with Asperger's Syndrome or ASD. Another layer of complexity may be added when one parent (or both parents) has Asperger's as well. With the child's diagnosis may also come thoughts about how ASD may affect siblings and other family members. Dealing with this information can be a delicate process for the entire family.

Parents with Asperger's

When you received your child's diagnosis, you probably endured a number of thoughts, feelings, and emotions. It may have been difficult to make sense of them at the time until you sorted them out and processed them through. As you learned more about Asperger's Syndrome, some of your thoughts might have begun to crystallize more clearly.

Among these thoughts may have been reflections of the diagnosis as it pertained to you and your own childhood, or that of your spouse. Were there times you endured growing up, or while attending school, that now have meaning? You may find that your child's diagnosis puts into perspective your experiences or makes sense of your spouse's quirks and idiosyncrasies. If your child's differences went unnoticed and undiagnosed until he was in his later childhood years, could it be because no one in your immediate family observed anything unusual about him? Was his way of being already firmly entrenched in your family's typical, ordinary, everyday-life way of being?

These are some of the thoughts you may be pondering, and they are not unusual. This chapter is a resource for mothers and fathers who are beginning to understand that their child's Asperger's Syndrome may be genetically inherited from one or both sides of the family.

COULD IT BE GENETIC?

As previously noted, little factual information is known about Asperger's Syndrome. For many, it is an invisible disability because it is so subtle it can go undetected. At present, statistics and other data are sparse, and you may speculate that there are any number of adults with Asperger's living and working in your community who are undiagnosed. One recent theory hypothesizes that certain types of people with "Asperger-like" traits—smart but antisocial—attract one another, leading to such couples bearing children with the same traits, only magnified due to an overload of genes. Dr. Fred Volkmar, a child psychiatrist at Yale University, estimates that Asperger's correlates with a genetic component more apparent than even autism. Dr. Volkmar suggests that about one-third of fathers or brothers of children with Asperger's show signs of Asperger's themselves, and there appear to be maternal connections as well. This information increases the likelihood that Asperger's may be present in your own family. Think about your child's lineage—are there, or were there, brilliant and creative but blatantly eccentric family members?

Depending upon your personality and the strength of your coping skills, this may be either relieving or disturbing information to consider. If the diagnosis is given and received with a "gloom and doom" mentality, you may lapse into a period of guilt or self-punishment. You may find yourself unjustly bearing the brunt of blame induced by yourself or your spouse. Parents of children with autism do tend to show increased stress associated with anxiety and depression when compared with parents of typical children. But remember, Asperger's is a naturally occurring experience and is no one's fault. Hopefully, this text will empower you to avoid believing negative Asperger's stereotypes in favor of focusing on the positives.

Psychologist Elaine N. Aron has developed a profile for individuals whom she distinguishes as "highly sensitive people." Her criteria are remarkably similar to traits in those with Asperger's Syndrome and may provide a gentle, less threatening basis from which to enter into a discussion about Asperger's in your family. Check out Dr. Aron's website and take her highly sensitive person quiz at *www.hsperson.com*.

CONFRONTING THE POSSIBILITY

For Dr. Liane Holliday Willey, author of the book *Pretending to Be Normal: Living with Asperger's Syndrome*, learning of her daughter's diagnosis was personally liberating because it wasn't until then that she realized she, too, had Asperger's. She defined the experience as reaching the end of a race to be normal. At long last, she embraced self-acceptance and was now in a position to articulate her sensitivities using the framework of Asperger's. Dr. Willey's journey was challenging, but fortunately her husband supported her. Regrettably, not all families handle the experience of recognizing Asperger's in themselves as well as this.

There are those marriages that simply do not sustain well under real or perceived pressures of raising a child with a different way of being. Families of children with Asperger's Syndrome are no exception. Educate and inform yourself and your spouse early on. Connecting with other parents in similar situations can dispel stigmatizing myths and stereotypes.

Recognizing Asperger's in Yourself or Your Spouse

If you find yourself suspecting that you or your spouse also has Asperger's Syndrome, please consider the following:

O Arm yourself with knowledge and gather as much information as you can from the Internet or the resources listed in this book.

O Broach the subject with your spouse by asking open-ended or leading questions that will provide opportunity for reflection, such as, "Do you think our child gets her love of science from your side of the family?"

O Because you are both still assimilating your child's experience, allow yourself and your spouse time to process this new twist on the situation.

O The conversations you have about Asperger's in the family should build slowly and incrementally.

O Avoid guilt, blame, and finger-pointing accusations such as, "It's all your fault our child is this way."

O Offer to explore and research Asperger's Syndrome with your spouse or to provide your spouse with whatever literature you've already gathered.

O Discuss marriage counseling or other professional supports in partnership with your spouse.

Understanding Asperger's as a probability for you and your spouse will be a learning time for you both. It can create marital stress and turmoil, or it can be an opportunity to strengthen and enhance your marriage.

You might be wondering, Is there an online resource for spouses if one or both are suspected to have Asperger's Syndrome? Yes. Asperger Syndrome Partners & Individuals Resources, Encouragement & Support, or ASPIRES, is a website for spouses and supporters of adults diagnosed (or believed to be) on the autism spectrum, with emphasis on problem solving within marriages and relationships. Check it out at *www.aspires-relationships.com.*

Sibling Relationships

Some families are remarkably resilient. Through unconditional love, they are able to persevere and meet new challenges while remaining whole and intact. Others seriously struggle or fall apart, and still others fall somewhere in between. Just as your family dynamics determine how your marriage will fare as you understand the significance of Asperger's for you and your spouse, so will your family makeup also determine how your child's brothers and sisters receive the same information. In other words, your children will take their cues from you and your spouse; the attitudes and actions you model will be reflected in them. They will not only project the attitudes toward their sibling's differences within the family, they will demonstrate these beliefs in school, the community, and the world at large.

SETTING A POSITIVE EXAMPLE
It is crucial that you work toward setting a positive tone when first presenting your child's Asperger's Syndrome to her brothers and sisters. It not only influences the quality of your immediate family relationships, but it also affects the ways in which your children perceive all people with differences for the rest of their lives.

When you broach the topic of Asperger's Syndrome with your child's siblings, consider these points:

○ Partner with your child about the issue of disclosure to agree upon how much or how little to reveal.

○ Decide if it's best to share the information with each sibling in privacy or if it should be done with the family as a group.

○ Begin by highlighting the ways in which people are more alike than different.

○ Discuss the gifts and talents of your other children first and then discuss those of your child with Asperger's.

○ Emphasize Asperger's as a natural experience and dispel fears about it being a contagious disease or something that can suddenly happen to just anyone.

○ Don't play the pity card—you want your kids to be kids and to maintain their typical relationships as brothers and sisters, not walk on eggshells.

○ Don't put unfair or unrealistic expectations on your child's siblings about increased responsibilities or the burden of future caretaking.

○ Do discuss the ways in which the entire family is going to strive toward being more sensitive to the needs of your child—needs previously unacknowledged or unrecognized.

○ Talk about respecting your child's ownership of confidentiality, discretion, and disclosure.

○ Allow for processing time and questions.

Finding a balance in how you love all your children is a fine art for any parent. It may be tough for your other children to see the kind of time you may invest with your child with Asperger's and not feel jealous or envious. Wherever possible, try to engage all your children in any activities that can include them all. If your child with Asperger's is receiving special instruction from an educator or therapist, are there games and routines that your entire family can take on? This will work toward family bonding, patience, and tolerance, and it will make learning fun for your child with Asperger's. The more you treat your child's way of being as natural and "no big deal," the more your child's siblings will automatically pitch in, help out, and pick up the slack without thinking or complaining beyond typical sibling bickering. The terrific ripple effect from this will be in how your children will grow to value diversity in all people.

HELPING SIBLINGS COPE

Still, there will be occasions when your child's siblings require your solid parental support when they are unable to manage or self-regulate internal or external pressures. Some pitfalls to be mindful of in observing your child's siblings may include coping with:

○ Manifestation of mental health issues due to the stress (self-imposed or imposed by you), especially in older daughters who may develop depression or an eating disorder

○ Perceived embarrassment caused by their sibling's way of being, especially in public

○ Being ostracized by peers who don't want to hang around them or come over to your house because of your child with Asperger's

○ Feeling perpetually pressured to "parent" or protect their sibling with Asperger's

○ Becoming weary and worn out from constantly defending their sibling

○ Feeling guilty when they want to go places and do things alone

○ Feeling pressured by peers to reject their sibling

Hopefully, none of these areas will manifest as concerns because you and your family have, from day one of the Asperger's diagnosis, set a positive, inclusive tone in relation to each family member's place in the home, school, and community. But if you should recognize problems in any of these areas, it will be important to have a private "powwow" with your child's siblings to offer your love, praise, and reassurances. Are there ways that you can compensate in partnership with your other children, especially if they've been feeling left out? Parenting is never set in stone; it changes from moment to moment. Be willing to admit it's true if you've inadvertently been neglectful. Plan some quality time with your child's siblings apart from the rest of the family. It may be rejuvenating for you all.

Creating an awareness for the importance of "family time" will be beneficial as your child's siblings take on other interests and broaden their circle of friends. Think of opportunities to engage everyone at least once a week in order to stay bonded. Examples could include a game night, planning and preparing a meal together, or participating in an outdoor activity. Regardless of what you do, it's the unifying experience that matters.

Extended Family

Revealing your child's Asperger's Syndrome diagnosis to extended family members is an issue of disclosure. Sharing such information should occur in partnership with your child in order to determine how much or how little others need to know.

DO THEY NEED TO KNOW?

In weighing your decision, consider the following:

O How often do you see these relatives?

O If you see them only once or twice a year, is it necessary to say anything?

O Can you foresee their reactions?

O If there's potential for gross misunderstanding, how will you handle that?

○ If they are intrigued and interested, how will you handle that without breaching your child's trust about disclosure (sharing more than what you agreed upon)?

○ Can extended family members be entrusted to honor disclosure?

○ Can they treat the subject with sensitivity and respect?

In the long run, the pros may outweigh the cons, but you and your child may decide it's simply no one's business at present. So many children with Asperger's can artfully "pass" and blend for the duration of a day with family that any differences may go completely unnoticed given all the other distractions. (Is it possible that your child comes across as downright complacent when compared with some of the more flamboyant children and adults at some of those gatherings?)

PREPARE FOR THEIR REACTIONS

If you decide it is appropriate to disclose information about your child's diagnosis, you may need to be prepared to deal with the potential for extended family members to show their ignorance (not a bad thing if they're open to education) or discomfort, or to overcompensate. You will need to consider how best to quell any situations that may arise from over-reactions should your extended family express concern about the entire family being stigmatized by the diagnosis. They may openly express hopelessness for your child's way of being, deluge you with literature that focuses on cures or "quick fixes," or, worse yet, confuse Asperger's Syndrome with some other diagnosis. Passive-aggressive behavior may transpire if extended family members become increasingly distant because of their own issues in processing the information, or if they want to spend time only with your other children. The worst-case scenario may be if they exclude or uninvite you and your child from future family get-togethers. A better scenario might be if they are overly cautious—trying not to do or say the wrong thing. In the latter situation, there is, at least, a way to offer assurances and education.

Hopefully, your wisdom and savvy as a mindful parent who is fast learning to be a strong and knowledgeable advocate will be of good service to you in setting the proper tone of sensitivity, respect, and unconditional love where extended family is concerned. In any case, to aid your child in surviving a day or more with extended family, you will wish to arm her with ammunition in the form of self-advocacy and coping skills prior to attending family gatherings.

You may be approached by friends and relatives who genuinely desire to learn more about Asperger's Syndrome. Hear them out and allow your intuition to guide you in how much you wish to be their single "point of contact" where all things Asperger's are concerned. You may want to let them borrow this book for starters or refer them to specific websites that you found of good service.

Agree upon the time duration of being there (and stick to it!), and ensure that your child has some materials related to her passion to quietly indulge in if she feels overwhelmed. Also be certain to locate an area where your child can retreat, undisturbed by others, to recuperate during much-needed downtime. Show her where it is and assure her that she may use it at will. Check with your family members in advance to find out what materials your child may access with their permission. Then, make sure your child knows where books, TV or videos, crayons, pen or paper, and Internet access can be found for solitary downtime activities. Other strategies that will be of enormous benefit in such situations will be discussed in detail later in this book.

Your Community

Sharing information about your child with neighbors, acquaintances, or total strangers in your community is no different than the process of determining when, where, and how to share the same information with family. Weigh carefully the drawbacks and positives that may come from sharing this information. It is an issue of disclosure that you should discuss in advance with your child in order to be as considerate and respectful of her feelings as possible. As before, ideally, your child should be encouraged to be her own advocate as early as possible in order to decide how much or how little to tell others about her way of being, if it's even necessary at all.

Some parents find themselves exasperated and embarrassed by their child's public meltdowns. They may garner stares, raised eyebrows, whispers, or flat-out denouncements of "Why can't you control your child?" There are those who decide to forego discretion and bluntly address gawking onlookers by revealing their child's diagnosis right there, on the spot. They may pass out "For Your Information" business-size cards that state, "My child has ASD and this is what you might see," followed by a list of meltdown behaviors or behaviors others might find quite peculiar.

You may find yourself in the position of these parents who want to educate others and simply want a little patience and understanding in the moment. But are you best serving your child by revealing such intimate information, or are you fueling misperceptions and stereotypes—especially if you explain, "This is Asperger's Syndrome" at the height of your child's public meltdown? Aren't you, in effect, sending a message to the community that "This is what Asperger's Syndrome looks like"? You know Asperger's Syndrome encompasses many things, and your child's inability to endure certain environmental stimuli is but one sliver of who she is as a human being. Think of the impressions people take away with them after being told, "This is Asperger's Syndrome." Would you want to be regarded in this way when you know you aren't at your best and you're coping the best way you know how?

As you are becoming more mindful through an awareness of parenting in the moment, is it possible for you to be a resource to others? There are probably parents in your community who are in need of understanding how to finesse their child-rearing style in a "conscious parenting" approach. In this way, you become an advocate for others.

We're all human, and as the parent of a child with a different way of being, your nerves will fray and are bound to wear thin. But before you vent your frustration or express your extreme dissatisfaction with your child's conduct, ask yourself:

O Am I being fair?

O Am I making this an issue about Asperger's?

O Am I disclosing information publicly out of anger?

O Have I been clear in giving my child concrete, visual information in advance about my expectations?

If you believe you've been fair, then remember to focus on addressing your child's behavior in the community as inappropriate to the environment, instead of making it about Asperger's Syndrome.

Important Points to Consider

Family dynamics are a balancing act in any family but especially in families with a member who has Asperger's. There will always be disagreements, sibling rivalry, and issues with extended family, but when Asperger's enters the picture these matters take on a whole new level of complexity. Here are some important issues to keep in mind:

O If you or your spouse has Asperger's Syndrome and now your child has been diagnosed, remember that it is not a blame game. It is no one's fault that your child has Asperger's. Now is not the time to shut down and blame; now is the time for positive action for your child.

O Sit down and discuss Asperger's with your other children. Find a way you are comfortable with to share this information with them. Let them ask questions and listen to their concerns. This affects their lives too.

O Partner with your child about whether extended family members need to be told. Is your child comfortable with other family members knowing? Prepare your child for the myriad reactions family members might have, from good to bad.

O Weigh the advantages and disadvantages to disclosing your child's diagnosis in your community. While it may seem easier to do so, think about whether you are doing it in the best interests of your child.

 **CHAPTER 9**

Fostering Relationships

Because your child may have difficulty perceiving the ebb and flow of typical social interactions, he may feel uncomfortable or be pegged as socially "awkward" when it comes to conversation with his peers. Navigating the ins and outs of everyday communications can be an art for anyone. The social interaction skills you instill in your child now will have long-term benefits as he matures through adolescence and into adulthood. Learning how to develop social circles and relationships that can lead to friendships is important to your child's future successes and mental health stability. With your support, your child can grow to learn ways to improvise and improve the quality of those interactions.

Your Child's Interactions

When you consider your child as an individual with Asperger's Syndrome, how does he fare in social conversation? Some children may appear shy and withdrawn, rarely speaking unless spoken to. Others may dominate the conversation with lengthy discussions about their most passionate interests. Your child may reflect these traits at different times or generally fall somewhere in between.

The child who appears shy and withdrawn likely wants to feel welcomed and included by others but doesn't know where to begin. Similarly, the child who releases the equivalent of a verbal dissertation knows how to talk circles around that topic and may think that everyone has the same degree of interest such that they are spellbound. This child also doesn't realize the mechanics of social conversation.

The Dance of Reciprocal Flow

As metaphors and analogies help to enhance our understanding, consider that, in both instances, each child wishes to partake in the "Dance of Reciprocal Flow" (not to be confused with "The Electric Slide"). The first child is partnerless, awaiting an invitation to the dance. When the invitation doesn't come, he may feel hopeless. He may internalize these feelings, frustrated by not understanding others or himself. This may lead to a sense of guilt or blame, which could fuel depression. The second child has leaped into the dance without first having learned the steps. He, too, is partnerless but believes that all those present are his exclusive dance partners, available to him at any given moment. Both children are set up to be singled out for their differences and potentially stigmatized for not knowing the dance that most everyone else appears to have learned naturally by picking up on spoken and unspoken social cues.

Developing friendships means either learning the Dance of Reciprocal Flow (and some are more masterful dancers than others) or approximating it well enough that one blends nearly seamlessly during the time spent on the dance floor. It is a gradual process. No one masters the dance immediately; you improve and gain more confidence as you practice the dance steps. As you've learned, most children with Asperger's Syndrome assimilate information in ways that are concrete and visual.

As your child's instructor in the Dance of Reciprocal Flow, you will wish to map this out for him, similar to the way that some people learn to dance by following the black silhouetted footprints positioned on the floor. As they memorize the dance routine and position of each step, they make fewer and fewer missteps. The dance becomes more fluid, requiring less effort and less thought. Finally, the footprint outlines fade altogether. They are now visible only in one's consciousness, unseen by others. Some will require intermittent, periodic "polishing" to brush up on the dance steps; others will retain it always, permanently etched in their minds. The importance in learning the dance is to know when and where to buoy your partner so that you both work together to create one whole presentation.

How often have you had a friendship damaged, harmed, or extinguished altogether as a result of misunderstandings or misinterpretations of communication? It happens all the time, every day. You may have a natural advantage in having already learned how to adeptly discern slang and sarcasm, tempered with understanding body language, facial expressions, eye gaze, and the tone and timbre of voices. Remember, for many people with Asperger's, this must all be taught and learned systematically. For being more intrinsic than average, those with Asperger's tend not to assimilate such social nuances as fluidly or naturally as others for whom the same social conventions may come more easily.

A challenge is that, while everyone dances the dance, they've all had different instructors or role models. As such, each person approaches the dance with unique, individual style and flair, reflective of their personality. Some people may even improvise and break the rules, such as those with a penchant for interrupting conversation or talking with their mouth full of food or gum. These nuances make discerning appropriate conversational flow difficult, but it really is a matter of etiquette. Your child should never be faulted for being polite during conversation, even if it sounds a bit "stiff" or formal.

USING MUSIC TO TEACH

To poise your child for developing friends, you will wish to explain the Dance of Reciprocal Flow using a similar analogy—unless your child is passionate about dancing and would relate well. Another analogy that might be helpful in your child's understanding may include deconstructing your child's favorite song. Music can be extremely important to kids with Asperger's, and all music is based upon the principle of call and response. According to the song's composition, there is a time when one sings or plays an instrument; this is the "call." Then there are times to pause and remain silent in order to await the "response." It is similar to the way in which two-way conversation is supposed to work.

To solidify this concept, you will want to draw this with your child while you start and stop the song. Help him identify one singer or one instrument and represent that on paper. He may even wish to use different colors to differentiate the participants in the song. Break the song down into portions and assist your child in understanding how all the pieces flow through call and response. In the most basic example, think of "Frère Jacques." If sung in round style, the song begins with the initial call being echoed in a response as additional communication partners are gradually added in.

USING CARTOON CHARACTERS TO TEACH

Your child may respond well to understanding social conversation when his favorite TV cartoon characters are involved. Again, it will be best if you are in a position to start and stop the action in order to highlight good and inappropriate conversation styles.

Help your child to reinforce what he's just seen by drawing it out on paper. Suggest that you both modify the conversation a bit. It may be a good, objective opportunity to demystify a real-time social interaction that failed your child. Using cartoon characters to take on a similar situation is a nonthreatening way for your child to deconstruct the issues. When finished, you may ask, "Isn't this like what happened with you and

Visuals are very useful survival tools in learning for many children with Asperger's Syndrome. Your child may already enjoy drawing or creating computer art now. Often, kids fabricate elaborate characters and complex plots and scenarios. It might be good sense to build upon that when mapping or reviewing social interactions among real-life people known by you and your child.

Carly last Saturday?" Next, discuss ways your child might approach the situation differently if similar circumstances arise.

Other useful analogies to conversation may include observing how animals interact and envisioning their "voices," or using the concept of maps where streets and highways converge and intersect. As always, maximize the benefit by using words and pictures, reviewing the information routinely until it is no longer needed.

Conversational "Bag of Tricks"

Another way to get to know others with the goal of making friends is to have a "bag of tricks" consisting of conversation starters and enders. Developing a repertoire of such tricks or skills will be of lifelong good service. Many children with Asperger's have terrific rote memories if they are able to create images of situations to best "match" the conversation starter or ender. To begin, partner with your child to break down, in writing and pictures, lists for each area. Here are a few sample conversation starters:

○ Greetings like "What's up?" "How's it going?" or "Hey" are fine for interacting with typical peers.

○ More respectful greetings for teachers and other adults may include "Good morning (or afternoon, or night), Mr. Eschelman," or simply, "Hello" or "Hi."

○ "What did you do over the weekend?"

- "What did you watch on TV last night?"
- "What are you doing after school?"

Sample conversation enders may include:

- "I gotta go now."
- "I'll catch (or see, or talk to) you later."
- "Take it easy."
- "See you tomorrow (or tonight, or Monday)."

With your child, try coming up with additions to the list. What do favorite cartoon or TV characters use as conversation starters or enders that are socially acceptable and fit well on these lists? Talk about how no one "owns" these conversation starters or enders; anyone can use them. Your child will need to be prepared for what comes next should he not initiate a starter or ender.

FEEDBACKS AND "SLIP-INS"

Next, discuss and map out lists for conversation feedbacks and conversation "slip-ins." Conversation feedbacks are responses to conversation starters or enders initiated by someone else. Conversation feedbacks may include responding with a question in order to elicit more information from the other person. Think of it as constructing a building or a model of some structure. Each piece of the conversation can add layers to the foundation either person began. When the conversation changes topic, the process should begin anew—even if the building is uncompleted.

Still, there may be times when you don't know how to respond and a simple, affirming interjection will indicate that you're at least listening. Conversation feedbacks are always useful tools to fall back on whenever one is uncertain of what to say and may include phrases such as:

- "I don't know what that is; tell me more."
- "I never heard of that before; can you explain it better to me?"

O "That's really neat!" or "That's interesting!"

O "Cool!" or "Awesome!"

O "I'm sorry about that."

Conversation slip-ins are socially acceptable alternatives to interrupting conversation. Your child will need to appreciate, through words and images, that it is considered rude to interrupt in conversation, but there are ways to "slip in" without being rude. You and your child will wish to identify when this works best (usually during a conversation lull or when someone has stopped talking). Conversation slip-ins may include:

O "Is it okay if I say something now?"

O "Excuse me, please."

O "May I add to what you're saying?"

O "Pardon me for interrupting." (formal or professional setting)

Interestingly enough, many adults with Asperger's Syndrome concede their struggle to understand the flow of conversation. Some have said it's tough determining where to appropriately pause or interject. One man had no idea he was being rude by constantly interrupting others until a close friend gently brought it to his attention.

Some of these might be too formal for a child and would better suit a young adult. Perhaps you and your child can come up with others to add to this list. Once all the lists are in writing with images (or keyed into the computer), your child will be in a better position to practice these strategies in real-time situations. If you are very familiar with how you have both formatted or coded the information into imagery, you can support your child by discreetly coaching him to call up the proper analogy suited to the moment. (For example, "Remember, this is just like when Daphne told Scooby-Doo, 'Take it easy.'") Mistakes and unexpected circumstances are bound to arise, and these will require private and respectful debriefing to explain. With time, you and your child can modify and adapt his bag of tricks to become adept in the Dance of Reciprocal Flow.

Opportunities for Bonding

There is no guarantee that understanding how conversation flows will lead to friendships. As previously discussed, building upon your child's most passionate interests and connecting to others with the same, or similar, passions will usually foster a depth to the relationship beyond mere surface conversation. Where your child may need you is in fostering situations in which he can meet others who are equally impassioned. Once connected with at least one other peer who "gets" him and speaks the same language, your child will feel terrific. Knowing that others value what he has to offer will bolster his self-esteem. There is no better way to feel bonded with others than through mutual love of something or someone.

FINDING OPPORTUNITIES

What opportunities are available in your community by which you can support your child in making contacts to build upon his passion for insects, astronomy, Japanese animation, or other topics? If you are uncertain, start by pursuing the following:

○ Programs and special events offered by your local library

○ Community projects or special celebration days

○ Opportunities offered through the newspaper, local circulars, or "merchandiser"-type papers

○ Opportunities offered through local television and radio stations

○ Community classes such as arts and crafts, or martial arts

- After-school activities sponsored by your school district
- Programs and special events offered by your local historical society or museums
- Special events sponsored by local athletic leagues

You may find other venues in your community to add to this list. As noted before, one of the most powerful and advantageous ways to connect with others with similar passions is through the Internet. The possibilities are endless. Your child may learn more about other kids of the same age, beyond just the passion they share, by locating them on a map and learning about the local industry, economy, and more. The child passionate about Japanese animation may even have the chance to communicate with someone of that culture. They can compare notes and exchange ideas about the video games each is developing.

SOCIAL "PRACTICE" GROUPS

In some communities, parents and professionals have banded together to form meeting groups for kids with Asperger's Syndrome. These gatherings provide a forum for unconditional acceptance in a safe and comfortable environment. Such groups do not advocate exclusion from typical children; rather, they are an opportunity for some children to learn social skills in a place where it's perfectly acceptable to mess up as you learn and practice.

One such social group for kids was initiated in Cherry Hill, New Jersey, in the spring of 2003. The Friendship Club was begun by a group of interested parents wanting activities and resources for their children with Asperger's. The program is sponsored through the Jewish Family and Children's Service of Southern New Jersey and staffed by parents, educators, and therapists.

The group meets weekly, teaching socially accepted rules and skills through role-playing games and worksheets. The lessons may involve comprehending that it's okay to make mistakes, dealing with teasing from others, or learning how to take "no" for an answer without melting down. The Friendship Club also emphasizes practicing eye contact and turn-taking in conversation. Posted rules and goals aid the children in staying focused when they require visual reminders.

Your local school district or county human services program may be able to tell you if any such meeting group already exists in your town or a neighboring town. If there is no such gathering group in your community, you may wish to consider establishing something similar in your area.

Finding Allies

When your child becomes an independent adult, you want him to know how to surround himself with good, honest, and trustworthy people who will be kind and understanding of his different way of being. Such folks will be there for your child (and vice versa) unconditionally to aid him in navigating real life when he needs it. Professionals in your child's life may come and go. An ally is someone not paid to be a participant in your child's life and who is there for the long haul. Empowering your child to identify the qualities that make a strong, reliable ally is paramount.

Allies may include siblings (without external, parental pressure to be caregivers), extended family, neighbors, friends, and members of the clergy. An ally may even be someone in a romantic context, the person who in your child's young adult or adult life becomes his partner or spouse. Of course, there are no guarantees that an ally will remain a permanent fixture—people move, change jobs, divorce, or drift apart. But ally relationships tend to be long-standing personal investments.

Your child's closest allies should be immediately apparent to you. They are those to whom he naturally gravitates and who welcome him unconditionally. Can you accept that, despite being a parent, you may not be considered by your child to be an ally? Allies should be natural—not forced—relationships in order for them to endure.

The qualities found in long-term allies may include someone who:

○ Accepts your child just as he is

○ Is patient, sensitive, and loving

○ Makes the time to be present with your child

○ Returns phone calls and e-mails promptly and reliably

○ Is interested and intrigued by your child's passions

○ Is willing to apply his or her own life experiences and expertise to the relationship with your child

○ Believes your child is a beautiful, gifted human being with lots to offer the world

Some kids with Asperger's relate better to adults. Because your child may portray himself as adult-like in his use of conversational language and interests, he may be treated as an equal and indulged by other adults. Your child may already have a strong rapport with one or more of your adult friends. This is okay—relationships are relationships; don't knock it. While you and your child continue to seek opportunities to connect with same-age peers, do not discourage your child from developing relationships with adults (unless you suspect their motives to be impure). If you seek to squelch those relationships simply because of age differences, it could be devastating to your child. Weigh your child's relationships with adults with your comfort level and allow your intuitions to guide you.

Is It Okay to Be Alone?

It is a stereotype that people with Asperger's Syndrome want to live solitary lives and deliberately isolate themselves from society in hermitlike existence. As more children are recognized to have Asperger's, there is a broadening awareness of the diversity among all people.

Remember the phrase "inherently gentle and exquisitely sensitive"? When one is bombarded daily by sensory stimuli that is irritating or painful, or when one is challenged to decipher the logic and rationales of others, it can become physically, mentally, and emotionally exhausting. We all relish our downtime—those fleeting opportunities when we can change into comfortable clothes, relax, and reward ourselves for having made it through another day. The child with Asperger's is no different, but his desire to be alone can be perceived as "abnormal" simply because the clinical diagnosis says so.

As a parent, you will wish to set rules for all your children about free time versus time you expect chores and homework to be accomplished. It is likely that your child with Asperger's loves nothing more than becoming deeply absorbed in his most passionate of interests—reading, drawing, Internet surfing, or watching TV. Ask that he abide by the rules you have agreed on, but don't penalize him for losing track of time unless you have just cause to believe it is deliberate. Be cautious of imposing your own biases about how long is "too long" to spend alone. (If you suspect your child might be experiencing a symptom of depression, then you will notice his need to withdraw becomes more and more pronounced.)

Many people cope with everyday stressors by indulging in their own personal relaxation techniques and routines, free from the demands of others. You may consider it "my time." Some people exercise, soak in a hot tub, read, or watch TV. We are all more alike than different, yet often parents and professionals place demands upon children as soon as they come through the door from school.

You may also have expectations about what being "social" should look like. But "social" should be defined differently for each individual, depending on that person's needs. You may value many friends as a mark of being socially successful. Some people with Asperger's are content with just a very few, select friends. Many are not social butterflies, don't wish to be, and never will be. Unless they wish to endeavor to become more social, such individuals may simply be the kind of folks who are completely comfortable with a small group of close-knit people. As a parent, you can arrange to expose your child to a variety of people within a range of environments and circumstances. Your child will guide you to those with whom he feels connected and wishes to know better.

Important Points to Consider

As a conscious parent, you always have an eye out for opportunities to bond with your child, and because you know him so well it comes naturally. But for your child with Asperger's, bonding with others is not always an easy task. Luckily you can help. Here are some things to keep in mind:

O Help your child understand the "dance" of conversations and practice with him. Create some helpful fallback lines that your child can use to start or end a conversation.

O Help your child seek out others who share his passions. There will be many opportunities to talk and bond over a familiar and loved subject.

O Understand that your child need allies in life and that despite your close relationship you might not be the ally he chooses. This is okay! You want your child to grow and become independent and you can't allow hurt feelings to get in the way. Be glad he has found a person he identifies with.

O Let your child be alone sometimes. All people like alone time; your child with Asperger's is no exception. In fact, being bombarded with stimulation all day can be exhausting for someone with Asperger's, and being alone may be just the right medicine.

CHAPTER 10

Educational Programming

Your focus on your child has made you a keen observer of her individual needs, but the range of professionals who support your child's education must also have a working understanding of her needs. Without such collaboration, your child may face social and educational challenges in a typical school environment. Wherever possible, children with Asperger's Syndrome should be fully included with their same-age peers in regular classrooms. In an inclusive environment, your child may enjoy the opportunity to grow socially and academically.

Your Child's School Experience

One distinct advantage to obtaining a formal Asperger's Syndrome or ASD diagnosis for your child is that she will be eligible to receive certain educational services and supports. One reason school districts are sometimes unable to provide such services is because the child has not been identified as needing support services. In some instances, even if educators are aware of your child's diagnosis, some may misinterpret your child's individual attributes. Sometimes children with Asperger's are accused of being "lazy," inattentive, or simply not applying themselves to the best of their abilities. This may be true in some children (as it may be for any neurotypical child), but such accusations have become so overused that they are Asperger's stereotypes. In other examples, schools may overlook the child who maintains his composure during the day (by being quiet or compliant) but has legitimate educational needs.

Other children, who are fine academic achievers but experience meltdowns during the day, may be "missed" by school districts as students needing a select educational program. Instead, such students may be placed in classrooms for children with emotional disturbances.

Such placements may be truly harmful to the child with Asperger's. In one instance, a child was set up to fail and the self-fulfilling prophecy was perpetuated. This particular fifteen-year-old had Asperger's and was extremely sensitive to touch. One day he was very upset about not receiving his report card when he expected it. When his teacher touched his shoulder, he reacted by striking her. The school resisted the Asperger's Syndrome diagnosis in favor of (inappropriately) placing the boy in a classroom for emotionally disturbed students.

Individuals with Disabilities Education Act

A safeguard to ensure that your child's educational needs are met by your school district is the Individuals with Disabilities Education Act, known as IDEA. (In this instance, the word "disabilities" is a necessary evil, and it shouldn't define how you or the world views your son or daughter.) IDEA is the federal law that guarantees your child's entitlement to a Free and Appropriate Public Education (FAPE). The types of disabilities covered by IDEA include the following:

O Autism

O Mental retardation

O Hearing impairment (including deafness)

O Speech or language impairment

O Visual impairment (including blindness)

O Serious emotional disturbance

O Orthopedic impairment

O Traumatic brain injury

O Other health impairment

O Specific learning disability

The last bullet, "specific learning disability," may apply to your situation if your child "does not achieve commensurate with his or her age and ability levels," or if your child "has a severe discrepancy between achievement and intellectual ability" in one or more of the following areas:

O Oral expression

O Listening comprehension

O Written comprehension

O Basic reading skills

O Reading comprehension

O Mathematics calculation

O Mathematics reasoning

These are all areas identified by IDEA (specifically in the Code of Federal Regulations, 34 C.F.R., section 300.341). As you can see, many children with Asperger's may readily qualify for educational support—especially the comprehension portions—based upon the breakdown definition of "specific learning disability." Other school districts may use the designation of "other health impairment" to qualify a child with Asperger's. This is where a comprehensive evaluation by a psychologist, psychiatrist, or other qualified professional experienced in diagnosing Asperger's Syndrome will be most helpful. The school district should offer to provide such an evaluation if you do not already have a diagnosis for your child. If not, the process can be initiated at your request. Ensure that you make this request in writing, include language giving your consent to an evaluation, and retain a copy for your records.

The conclusions of the professional conducting the evaluation will likely show discrepancies between your child's intellectual abilities and her ability to achieve in any of the previously listed areas. This is vital in order for your school district to appropriately qualify your child for an educational program designed to meet her needs. (Districts are mandated to have "Child Find" policies in effect to identify, locate, and evaluate children who may be protected under IDEA.) In this way, you can begin to establish a proactive, working partnership with your school district.

A comprehensive evaluation by a professional experienced in identifying Asperger's Syndrome should also contain recommendations for how you and your child's educational team might move forward in developing a plan to support your child.

Developing a Plan

The evaluation for your child should determine her special education (or related service) needs and will generate an appointment for a team meeting to develop an Individualized Education Program (IEP). The IEP is the document that will detail, in writing, an individualized approach to meeting the unique needs of your child. The team should include:

O You and your spouse

O One regular education teacher

○ One special education teacher

○ A school representative who can make decisions about the delivery of services (usually the school principal)

○ Someone who can interpret the evaluation results as they apply to your child's educational instruction

○ Other participants with special expertise or knowledge of your child

Your child may also participate if she chooses to be present.

Participants with special expertise may include a parent advocate knowledgeable about IDEA and the IEP process, a professional consultant who specializes in developing IEPs, or a professional consultant who specializes in Asperger's Syndrome. Finding a specialist can be a crucial issue, and it can be frustrating to both parents and school officials when one is not accessible.

At this point (and depending upon your geographic location), it may not be realistic to expect that a teacher experienced in educating students with Asperger's Syndrome will be teaching your child. Because you know your child best, you may become fiercely protective of and defensive about what you believe she needs. On the other hand, most willing and cooperative school districts may lack such expertise and may be of the position that they are doing all they can. Such disputes are addressed later in this chapter.

THE EVALUATION PROCESS

If you have requested that your school district evaluate your child, the district must comply, and this process should be completed within sixty days after your first written request. After this, the district will ask that you sign a "Permission to Evaluate" form. The evaluation should be completed within sixty days after your original written request (which contains consent from you to evaluate your child), not sixty days after you've signed the permission form. Once the evaluation is completed, a team meeting should be convened to review the evaluation. You should receive your child's evaluation well in advance of the team meeting, but no later than ten days prior to such a meeting. This team meeting may also serve as the first IEP meeting if you wish.

Don't hesitate to request an advance blank copy of the tool that will be used to evaluate your child. It will help you understand the special education services process and provide indicators of areas in which your child may excel or fail. One excellent website with information on special education law is *www.wrightslaw.org*.

If your child has been deemed eligible for services, IEP team members should be identified, and the first meeting should occur within thirty calendar days of the original determination of eligibility. The completed IEP must then be implemented within ten school days. It must also be reviewed yearly and can be revisited in a team meeting upon your request outside of the annual meeting date. The IEP must also be in effect for your child at the beginning of each new school year.

Creating the Individualized Education Program

The initial IEP meeting is the time and place to develop the document that will be the blueprint for your child's educators. The draft document should be transcribed into the final document immediately after the meeting. It should include:

O A cover sheet with a sign-in page listing all participants

O An acknowledgment of your child's eligibility

O An area for you to sign, acknowledging that the school district has provided you with a copy of your rights during the process, known as "procedural safeguards"

O Basic information such as your contact numbers and address, your child's date of birth, and her anticipated year of graduation

- A list of "special considerations," such as visual or hearing impairment, behaviors that impede your child's ability to learn (or that of classmates), and communication issues

- A summary of your child's strengths (her passions and interests)

- A summary of your child's needs (those areas in which she requires special support)

A strong IEP team should be able to find a balance between your child's strengths and needs. Too often, such meetings can focus upon issues that others may perceive as "behavioral" or emotional disturbances. When this occurs, teams get sidetracked and lose their focus. Teams may digress and deteriorate. Parents may leave feeling angry or upset, and the self-fulfilling prophecy is perpetuated. For this reason, and particularly in very sensitive situations, it is advisable to have a professional in attendance who fits the bill of "other participants with special expertise or knowledge of your child." In partnership with the team, this person can help keep things focused on your child as a child first and foremost.

ESTABLISHING GOALS

The next step is to set IEP goals that are specific to your child's strengths and needs in order to track your child's educational progress and ensure that the team is implementing what it committed to doing. The goals should be realistically achievable for your child and written in such a way that they are easy to track or "measure," in order to see your child's growth and keep the team accountable. For example, an appropriate goal for a kid of any age with Asperger's might be in the area of developing computer skills (if she's not already a computer wizard). While this may sound rather generic, the spin here is to make it specific to your child's Asperger's. The purpose of the goal should be clearly stated, such as a goal for accessing the Internet: "The student will develop skills to use a computer to communicate, to gain information, and to increase social relationships independently three out of five times." Next, objectives to meet the goal should be identified in sequence. The sequence for the computer goal might look like this:

- The student will learn the functions of the computer, including turning the computer on, signing on to the Internet, and using the keyboard and other functions in order to explore her passions (such as searching for information about insects as they relate to a lesson plan).

- The student will create and access a file and store information she wishes to save in the file.

- The student will learn methods to participate in social interaction through electronic media (e-mail).

Be conscious and consistent in highlighting your child's valuable attributes in addition to whatever she requires to regulate herself each school day. This will influence others' perceptions of her while ensuring that her school team reflects on her needs pro-actively, encouraging a mindful accountability on the part of all.

A method and schedule of evaluation for each goal objective should also be included. For example, the method for the last objective listed might read, "During computer learning opportunities, the student will be afforded opportunity to increase social interactions by learning to use e-mail and other communication avenues."

A goal for enhancing self-advocacy might address your child's ability to identify and communicate her sensory sensitivities in the school environment. A goal or objective might read, "The student will be able to communicate in a socially acceptable manner the specific change she requires in her educational environment four out of five times." The method should include supporting the child to identify environmental stimuli that are irritants and detract from learning.

MODIFICATIONS OF PROGRAMS

The IEP should also list "program modifications and specially designed instruction" that may include elements incorporated into goal areas that team members should bear in mind. Such a useful list may include examples like:

- Limit or eliminate visual and auditory stimulation and distractions in the learning setting.

- Explain directions clearly, in steps and with visual representations.

- Allow extended wait time and processing time.

- Use photo depictions where possible instead of cartoons or drawings.

- Provide advance notice of schedule and special situations.

- Be consistent with the expectations established for the student.

- Provide an individual weekly schedule to follow.

The IEP document will also indicate the projected date for implementation of services, the anticipated duration of services, and any revision dates. Specifications addressing how the school district intends to report IEP goal progress should be clearly stated. There must also be a statement reflecting why your child's current educational placement represents an inclusive environment as fully as possible (called "least restrictive environment") as opposed to an alternative placement.

Resolving Disagreements

Some parents and school districts are possessed of more experience and greater expertise in educating children with Asperger's than others. There will always be kinks to iron out in the IEP process, and these can usually be addressed at the annual IEP meeting or at a requested reopening of the IEP. When parents encounter resistance from a school district it is usually because the district:

- Doesn't "see" your child's diagnosis as viable

- Believes your child's challenges to be exclusively behavioral issues

- Believes it is meeting the goals and objectives of the IEP to its best ability

When parents resist a school's efforts, it is usually because they are extremely frustrated that the school district doesn't understand Asperger's and, as a result, doesn't "get" how to educate their child. Ignorance can be used as an initial excuse, but it is not an acceptable long-term excuse. School districts have a responsibility to make provisions for the continuing education of teachers and to seek outside technical assistance and expertise as necessary. Parents have a responsibility to serve as an outlet concerning their child's strengths and needs, as well as to direct the district to viable resources and expertise wherever possible.

When the circumstances of educating your child through proper implementation of the IEP goals and objectives become less than satisfactory, you have recourse available to you, provided by the IDEA law. You may request an Impartial Due Process Hearing (in writing) at any point at which disagreement arises about the delivery of education to your child. This includes your child's identification, evaluation, or placement, or the implementation of the IEP.

Defending your child's educational rights may be stressful and exasperating. If you find yourself in such circumstances, try taking a mindful approach by ensuring you have times of solitude to reflect and regroup. It may also be useful to try perspective-taking by processing what it is you find to be confrontational about the situation and interpreting it from a different angle.

The Impartial Due Process Hearing takes place with an "impartial hearing officer." The hearing officer is the "fact finder" who hears all the evidence and makes a ruling on the issues presented during the meeting. Such individuals are employed by your state government's education office of dispute resolution and are of varied background and position, such as former education administrators, attorneys, or psychologists.

A hearing is to be held within thirty days of the request. The school district must forward a parent's request to the office of dispute resolution

If you are in conflict with your child's school district, you need not go it alone. Connecting with other parents who have "been there, done that" should be of enormous benefit in your endeavor. Some such parents, who have become quite savvy to special education law, may be available to support you in meetings as parent advocates. You may be able to locate such parent advocates through your local chapter of the Autism Society of America or other community autism groups, or by networking with other parents on social media.

within five days of its receipt by the district office. The hearing officer's decision must be issued within forty-five days of the request for the hearing.

Be advised that there are often delays in scheduling, or a hearing officer may not be timely in making his final determination to settle a dispute. During the dispute, the child in question is to remain in her current educational placement (unless she is a danger to herself or others). The hearing officer's decision may be appealed and taken to an appeals panel within thirty days. The appeals panel must render a decision within thirty days after the review request.

Hopefully, such measures will be entirely avoidable, but if a parent remains dissatisfied after exhausting local administrative avenues, action may be brought in any state court of competent jurisdiction or in any district court of the United States, as provided for in IDEA. There is no statute of limitations for commencing such action in federal court, but it is advisable to file as soon as possible. There may be time-frame limitations for filing a case in your state court.

Moving to file a case is stressful, frustrating, and draining for all parties involved. However, court rulings can set precedent for changes in law to the benefit of all. Any time significant change has occurred in how children with differences are educated, it has been at the instigation of passionate parents simply wanting fair and equal opportunities for their children.

Alternative Education Programs

Hopefully, you will be a persuasive advocate when interacting with your child's school district. You just may be the person to educate and enlighten the professionals in your district if they require a better understanding of Asperger's Syndrome. In some extreme instances, families have moved to another school district or another state in order to have their child attend a certain school program. Unfortunately, in addition to the stress on the whole family that this type of upheaval can cause, it also allows school districts to remain uneducated about how best to support students with Asperger's Syndrome.

CHARTER SCHOOLS

Most states have an educational option called charter schools, in which the school district has received a "charter" from the state. The charter provides rules, such as where the school is located and the maximum number of students permitted to attend. With a charter, the school district receives the funding and allocations based on the number of students. The state department of education grants the school district funding to pay for teacher salaries, equipment, and materials to meet the individual needs of each student in a charter school.

Charter schools are considered "public schooling" and must abide by all state regulations. The charter school may have an emphasis on the arts or science with a smaller teacher-student ratio.

VIRTUAL CHARTER SCHOOL

Another innovative program, called a virtual charter school, uses the charter school model with a couple of differences. The virtual charter school is like a "public school in a home environment," but it is not the same as home schooling.

Former U.S. Secretary of Education William Bennett and some others started a company called K12, headquartered in McLean, Virginia. K12 provides the curriculum and management services; the virtual charter school hires the teachers and support staff. The head of the school, the controller, and a few others are employees of K12.

To attend a virtual charter school, the student's parents unenroll him from the local school district and enroll him in the virtual charter school. The school district funding follows the student and encompasses books, materials for art and for science experiments, a computer, and other materials. The student also receives a regular education teacher, a special education teacher, and an IEP, just as in the local school district.

The teachers become the educational supports working in partnership with the parents (who have the lead) to educate the child and ensure she takes all the state-mandated standardized tests. The parent must log time daily on a website and track the student's progress, such as what lessons she has completed; lesson plans are also received via the website. Frequent field trips, all of an educational nature, are planned as a way for the children, teachers, and parents to connect with one another.

HOME SCHOOLING

Increasingly, parents of kids with Asperger's are choosing to home-school their children. This may be because they are dissatisfied with their child's school district, their child's curriculum, or issues related to their child's IEP. Some parents may feel they know best how to meet their child's educational needs, or they wish to afford their child individualized educational opportunities that build on passions and interests and provide one-on-one attention. In the most disconcerting circumstances, children with Asperger's may be home-schooled because they have been taunted and bullied by other students, or because teachers have misperceived them as "lazy" or devalued them as "underachievers."

Bernie Pippin, a teacher and guidance counselor, has been a home-school supervisor for many years, has been an evaluator for home-school families, and has home-schooled her own two children. She explains the home-school process based on her experience teaching in Pennsylvania, but advises that protocols may vary substantially from state to state. (If you are considering home-schooling you are advised to contact your state department of education or log on to your state's website for details.)

Pippin notes: "The superintendent of the school district in which the family resides has the responsibility for the supervision of a home-schooling program. When an initial decision is made to home-school a student, a parent, guardian, or other authorized person submits a notarized affidavit to the superintendent indicating the plan to home-school the student. The affidavit should be accompanied by a set of objectives that are to be worked on for that school year. This process may be done at any time in the initial school year; however, in subsequent school years August 1 is the deadline for submission."

According to Pippin, the school district is required to provide to the home-schooling family copies of the texts used by the students in the school who are in the same grade level as the home-schooled student. There is a wealth of curriculum offerings available to home-schooling families, as most major educational publishing houses have come to recognize the home-school market. Some families choose to invest in one curriculum and use it exclusively; other families pull resources from various places. The one substantial advantage to educating from a traditional home-schooling model is that the supervisor of the program has the flexibility to make decisions that she feels are best for the student and to use materials that are consistent with the needs and abilities of the student.

Pippin continues, "Throughout the school year the supervisor of the program should keep a record of the days of instruction and all the subjects logged by the student. Some use a plan book, some use a calendar or computerized log. The supervisor also should be consistently and regularly gathering examples of the work done by the student for the portfolio to be assembled for the end-of-the-school-year evaluation."

In addition, tutors may be accessed for various areas that the home-school supervisor doesn't feel qualified to teach. Private schools or educational institutions affiliated with religious denominations may offer a more individualized curriculum with one-on-one instruction, but the cost of enrolling your child may be prohibitive.

BENEFITS AND DISADVANTAGES

Alternate educational placements may benefit the child with Asperger's Syndrome through smaller teacher-child ratios, leading to more individualized attention and quality assurance in your child's learning comprehension. Smaller class sizes may afford instructors the luxury of time to focus attention on meeting the unique educational needs of each child. Educational curricula in alternate settings may also have greater flexibility and provide for enhanced opportunities to reinforce curricula in ways that may be tangible and concrete for the child with Asperger's, such as regular field trips to museums, businesses, landmarks, and other community attractions. There may also be opportunity for creative programming in which the child may have myriad choices from which to select when planning class projects, presentations, or reports. Greater individualized attention may also mean that your child's personal passions can be used to underscore her learning in ways that might prove difficult or impossible in larger public school classes.

A disadvantage to alternative educational programming and placement may be the cost. If a newly designed program is considered, planning, implementation, and start-up time are all factors that may be deterrents for some as well. Social opportunities may be more limited with smaller or one-student classes unless efforts are made to compensate for this. Your local school district or state department of education should be able to provide you with details about a range of education program options, as well as funding options and obligations in order for you to make an informed decision about where your child receives her education.

Important Points to Consider

If you want your child to have the same high level of focus and attention that you provide at home at her school, then you need to be an advocate for your child's rights. You should familiarize yourself with what will be required of you to get the best possible education for her, and though each state and school district might differ in requirements, there are certain things you should keep in mind:

- Under the Individuals with Disabilities Education Act (IDEA), your child is guaranteed a fair and appropriate education and your child's school is required to execute that plan.

- Your child's Individualized Education Program (IEP) will set goals for your child's education; your input about your child's behaviors and attributes will be invaluable toward making sure those goals are appropriate and attainable.

○ You may not be a seasoned educator but you know your child best, so do not allow yourself to be pushed into any decisions you do not think will be in your child's best interest.

○ If you are dissatisfied with the level of care at your child's school, you have the right to seek alternative schools or home-schooling.

School-Related Issues

During the school year, the majority of your child's time is spent in a school environment. It probably feels as though his teachers see him more than you do! As the expert on your child, it is important that you are in a position to suggest that certain adaptations and accommodations be made in your child's school environment. Identifying and addressing your child's needs while he is at school will create an atmosphere conducive to a successful balance between learning and socializing.

The School Day

School presents an environment in which children are expected to be attentive listeners and ready learners. In addition, the school day provides numerous opportunities for students to spend time getting to know one another. It will be important that you, your child, and your child's educators have a clear understanding of the most salient points of communicating with a child with Asperger's Syndrome (as discussed in Chapter 5). Specifically, how educators communicate information and the processing time they allot for it can make or break your child's ability to assimilate educational curriculum on a day-to-day basis. If your child is very passive or is a "pleaser," he may readily get swallowed up in confusion and misunderstanding—all the while giving the impression that everything's fine, until it's too late.

How Your Child Learns

It will be crucial to communicate with your child and his educators, preferably prior to the start of the school year, in order to clarify your child's needs. Do his teachers have a clear understanding of what his needs will be (perhaps as dictated by the IEP), and does your child know what to do and say if he gets "stuck"? If you know your child to be a strong visual thinker and learner, ensure that any verbally communicated curriculum is reinforced with visuals. Some children cannot process visual and auditory input simultaneously without distraction; they are "mono-channel," meaning they cannot absorb what they are seeing and hearing at the same time and can attend to only one or the other. As many children with Asperger's Syndrome are so visual, this means there is potential for them to be distracted by everything in the room, so that they absorb only bits and pieces of the instruction.

In one instance, a young boy's school team members were frustrated because they thought they were supporting him fully by assigning him a classroom aide. However, the aide was verbally reiterating the classroom teacher's direction in such a way that their words overlapped. The boy was receiving almost exclusively verbal instruction, out of sync, and in stereo! Now, consider his predicament in desiring to pay attention to his teacher, but knowing he must also attend to his aide. Layer on top of that the constant motion of a typical elementary school classroom setting, and it was a recipe for disaster.

YOUR CHILD'S STRENGTHS

Many children with Asperger's Syndrome generally possess a number of strengths upon which educators may build. These include:

O A strong knowledge base for individual topics of passionate interest

O The desire to conform to rules and boundaries

O Retaining information best when it is visual, sequential, and linear

O Best understanding logical, concrete topics of discussion

O A willingness to please and to keep trying

> Your child may well benefit from a classroom aide in order to support his comprehension. It will be best—and nonstigmatizing—if all the children in class understand that the aide is accessible to them if they have questions or need guidance to reinforce the teacher's instruction. In this way, the aide's role is discreet.

It will be important that your child's educators embrace the concept of building upon your child's passions (as discussed in Chapter 7). It is unrealistic to expect a classroom teacher to center educational curriculum around one child's passions; however, where doing so is possible, it will help engage the child if the teacher can artfully introduce elements of the passion(s) in the instruction. Strategies for linking passions to learning opportunities are best applied by your child's classroom aide or directly by you if no aide is assigned or available. All children are eventually confronted with educational concepts that are vague and indiscernible for them. Connecting passions in the way described in Chapter 7 is intended to occur outside of the classroom setting and, ideally, before and after the confusing assignment. Your job and that of the teacher (and aide) is to "coach" your child on the sidelines before sending him out into the game. That is, deconstruct the concept with which he is struggling by using his passion both before and after he's expected to learn and retain it.

For example, you might suggest that the names given to parts of plants also relate to the hanging vines in a Mario Bros. computer game. Instead of asking that your child recite the textbook plant parts, request that he link the same information to the Mario Bros. plants. He will retain this information and, with a gentle reminder, will "call up" the knowledge when it's required (such as at test time).

Some children take this to extremes and don't realize they are sidetracking a teacher's instruction with lengthy explanations of their passions (which can fuel educators to stereotype the passions). Children who do this need clear, concise, and written rules provided to them about when and where it's okay to expound upon their interests.

LEARNING BY DOING

Your child likely has a strong associative link when learning. That is, he learns on the spot, in the moment while "doing" whatever it is, and will forever retain and "link" that experience with the moment. (You've done this, too, by the way you can recall distinct details about your child's birth, a parent's passing, or even the events of 9/11.) Many children with Asperger's think and learn this way. It will be important, then, to understand your child's struggles if educators wish to place emphasis on "pull out" programs or classes in which your child works one-on-one with an adult with the expectation that he process, retain, and apply what was just learned to the classroom situation. The two rarely mesh with success because of the strong associative link.

Your child will be poised for greater success if he can learn by doing in the moment and through incorporation of as many visuals as possible to reinforce it. In so doing, a visual "imprint" is recorded in his memory that, with gentle prompting, he can call up and replay. You may then incrementally build upon such pleasing experiences by relating them to something new and different. For example, you might suggest to your child, "Remember when we made homemade peanut butter?" (Give him

> When in doubt about how your child may best think and learn, think back on your own experience with "associations." Recall how certain scents or songs are forever linked in your memory to people, places, and life events and may be inseparable from those recollections.

processing time to replay the mind movie.) Then continue, "The way a factory processes sugar cane is similar because . . . ." You may be surprised at the quality of detail with which your child is able to relay information. He may become excited about taking a pleasing, fun learning experience and applying it to something novel.

Environmental Issues

Schools are fraught with environmental stimuli that can conspire to wreak havoc on your child's sensory sensitivities. Many children with Asperger's already torture themselves with anxiety about wanting to follow the rules, live up to teacher expectations, and get through each day without incident. In addition, they must grapple with having their senses assaulted throughout the day. In some instances—if the child is not yet a self-advocate, or if he is unaware of his own sensitivities—he may be unable to pinpoint exactly what triggers him to lose control. This is extremely common.

So many kids with Asperger's Syndrome are keenly aware of the social, educational, and environmental expectation that they blend in and "fit in." To compensate, they "hold it together" all day long as best they can. Once they get home, they finally release, lose control, and melt down in the safety of the home environment—where they feel most comfortable to let down their guard. This creates a perplexing situation for teachers who report to parents that their child seems "fine during the day." It also creates a frustrating situation for parents who may internalize their own self-doubts about something they must be doing wrong. It is no one's fault; the child is merely reacting to the relief at dropping the façade he's borne for the past six hours or more.

Be understanding about your child's need to unwind after school. While it may be frustrating to you, always feeling that you are getting the brunt of the emotional issues at home, try to see it from your child's point of view. At home he finally feels safe to let go. Giving him the freedom to do so, within reason, will be cathartic for him.

Here are a number of suggestions that you will wish to share with your child's teachers to minimize the potentially hurtful environmental stimuli in typical school settings:

O Hallways can become extremely noisy and "echoey." Wherever possible, keep classroom doors shut.

O The volume of the PA system in the room may be too loud. If it's possible to adjust the volume, this can help. Same for the change-of-class bell.

O Classroom walls can be overstimulating and "busy" with decoration. If visuals cannot be streamlined, at least keep them somewhat static so the child with Asperger's can become accustomed to them.

O Consider felt pads under the feet of all classroom chairs as buffers against the constant scraping noise they make.

O Carrels or partitions around learning stations and computer centers are great for creating visual blocks on both sides of a student and can also cut down some noise.

O Ringing classroom phones can be startling. Switch to a flashing light instead of a ring to indicate a call.

O Classroom announcements or posters like "Ten Great Ways to Treat Others" are most effective if transcribed and distributed to all kids (this makes them easier to retain when outside the room).

O Numbering classroom rules as written reminders for the child with Asperger's is a good idea, but publicly displaying them on a desktop is stigmatizing. Tape them inside a child's notebook or binder and refer to them discreetly.

O Focus on natural lighting instead of fluorescent lights when possible, using fewer overhead lights or adding alternate lighting such as floor lamps.

O Give the child with Asperger's advance notice of fire-drill times so that he may brace himself for the noise. If he cannot tolerate it, small foam earplugs may help, or wearing iPod earbuds may diffuse the noise.

O Ensure that all students have advance knowledge of schedule changes outside of the routine, such as early dismissal or assemblies.

You may be pleasantly surprised to learn that many environmental adaptations and accommodations can be low in cost or cost nothing. In fact, you may wish to apply them, wherever possible, to your own home in addition to those of friends, neighbors, or relatives.

Implementing these measures will significantly help the child with Asperger's to "hold it together" in a more environmentally friendly atmosphere. (And, no, don't allow yourself to feel as if it's "coddling" your child—doesn't it make sense to poise him for success instead of set him up for failure in the school environment, where he spends the majority of his day?)

Homework

When you are young and extremely sensitive, school is your life, teachers are omnipotent, and homework is everything. Many children with

Asperger's Syndrome generate undue stress for themselves by agonizing over homework to the point that they cannot be calm and rest because they feel so overwhelmed. Some may wail, cry, or hyperventilate because they believe homework to be a life-or-death situation. Parents and teachers may affirm that they know the child is capable of the work; however, this is not about incapability. The child with Asperger's Syndrome can be overcome with stress and anxiety by a litany of tasks that seem insurmountable. Being confronted simultaneously with homework, impending tests, and assignment due dates may fuel such a tremendous sense of frustration and futility that the child may be totally unable to discern where even to begin.

PROBLEMS WITH HOMEWORK

If your child becomes upset and overwhelmed when confronted with multiple homework assignments, he will require your support to break down the tasks (organized visually on a timetable that becomes the child's property) so that the assignments are scheduled in manageable portions. Reinforce that the child need focus only on the work scheduled for the allotted time slot. Your child's teacher will be an invaluable resource in helping to "map out" such a timetable into realistically doable bits.

A child's confusion and misunderstanding of directions can lead teachers inaccurately to label that child for his "behaviors." Their observations may focus upon some children's inability to complete homework. The refusal to complete a homework assignment in full may stem from the child feeling personally offended by what is being asked of him. If your child has demonstrated that he can master a concept, he may become offended when asked to demonstrate that capability by essentially "regurgitating" the same concept in various ways (via the homework). A compromise may be to allow the child to do fewer homework problems.

If the homework is going to be publicly reviewed aloud in class, parents and teachers will need to be more creative in conveying why completing the entire assignment is necessary. Or teachers could arrange to stagger the order of the assigned homework problems, with both student and teacher being aware of which problems he is most likely to be called upon to report.

PERFECTIONISM AND ANXIETY

Some children operate in a "perfection mode" because they are "pleasers." They may relate better to adults with more advanced skills, or they torture themselves trying to duplicate computer-generated examples in textbooks, like perfect handwriting, for example. Trying to be as perfect as adults appear to be only magnifies the self-imposed pressure to comply with exacting accuracy. Tension and anxiety can balloon out of control for the child who must erase his work over and over again because it doesn't "match" the textbook or teacher's example.

If your child does this, he needs you to express, in writing and pictures, an understanding that everyone messes up and does things wrong every day. It may come as a groundbreaking revelation for your child to learn that his parents, teachers, relatives, doctors, and others don't do everything exactly right all the time. This is not giving him permission not to strive to do his best; it's a discussion about flexibility within rules and permission for him to go easy on himself. Your child will likely be absolutely tickled to hear your own stories about the times you messed up in school and lived to tell about it!

With patient support and practice, these homework strategies should help your child relax and focus.

Bullying

Like it or not, many kids with Asperger's are perceived as different by their peers despite their efforts to blend and assimilate. Coming across as different can make a child a target in the eyes of those who prey upon the weak and defenseless. Many children with Asperger's become terrified and anxiety-ridden at the prospect of being bullied, especially during the transition to middle school and high school. As freshmen, they are younger than the other students, who may traditionally give all incoming students a hard time.

WHEN THE BULLY IS A STUDENT

Many school districts have taken a no-tolerance approach to bullying, especially with the significant increase in school violence nationally in recent years. They have also developed written rules and guidelines about what is unacceptable student behavior and the consequences for not complying with the rules. Your child should receive such a written policy either in advance of the start of school or within the first week of school. If you don't have it, contact the school to request it or you may locate the information posted directly to the school district's website. Having it may help soothe and appease your child's worries.

Facilitating partnerships that may lead to friendships (allies) will be critical, starting at an early age. Some schools also have a buddy system, whereby younger students are mentored or assisted by older, supportive students during an orientation period. You may also need to partner with your child to devise a way to hold a frank discussion with his teachers about the need for protection during the school day. Appropriate ways to cope with verbal and physical abuse need to be taught and rehearsed. Give your child a numbered list of actions to discreetly maintain in the event of an incident. The actions may include the exact phrases to use when telling his abuser to stop it and knowing to whom bullying should be reported. Some children may also require coaching to learn how to recognize some forms of bullying that may be very subtle, such as the student who was coerced by his bullies into swearing at a teacher and then bore the brunt of the punishment alone.

Providing your child with your school's written policy on bullying is not enough. He needs to know exactly whom he may trust to approach and confide in (which should be any adult in the school).

Luke Jackson, a young man with Asperger's, has commented on bullying in his writings:

> Being different may not be a problem for me, or other kids like me, but it sure seems to cause problems for "normal" (ha!) kids. The result . . . bullying! I think there is some amount of bullying going on at all times, in schools everywhere. Some have it worse than others, but all have it. I was definitely bullied, and "it" was very painful at times. Always remember that "different is cool!" A lot of teachers and adults

think bullying is "part of growing up," but I have written books, talked at conferences, and opened my life up on television just to let everyone know that people with autism in any shape or form are just as entitled to be themselves as anyone else in the world.

WHEN THE BULLY IS AN ADULT

In some unfortunate instances, the bully is not another student but an insensitive teacher. One teenage girl with Asperger's honestly did not understand her gym teacher's instructions. After telling her several times (still in ways the student did not understand), the exasperated teacher pushed the girl and said, "What are you? A retard?" This is, of course, inexcusable behavior and must be dealt with by counseling the child immediately to prevent the onset of post-traumatic stress disorder. The issue also needs to be addressed with the school administration so that the child is removed from that teacher's class and the teacher's behavior is addressed.

You may also need to counsel your child about reporting extreme cases of bullying; ensure that he is clear about what is good-natured kidding and what is unacceptable to endure. It can be a fine line sometimes, and sorting it through will be an ongoing process.

Unstructured School Environments

Many children with Asperger's thrive during those portions of the school day that are structured by routine. Yet those same students may socially flounder during the many unstructured school events that occur throughout the day. These include:

O Recess

O School assemblies

O Hallway socializing between classes

O Gym class

O Lunchtime

O Riding the bus to and from school

Your child may also benefit greatly from having a repertoire of conversation starters, enders, and slip-ins. Wherever possible, your child will be best poised to weather the awkwardness of unstructured school situations if he can volunteer for, or be assigned, a responsibility or role during the activity. For example, many kids with Asperger's are not as physically graceful as they'd wish to be. Playing on a team in gym class can get confusing and uncomfortable, but this can be tempered if he is also in charge of keeping score.

Nowadays, it is entirely acceptable for all kids to spend downtime engaged in inconspicuous, solitary activities like reading, privately listening to music on an iPod, or playing small, handheld computer games to maintain focus. Determine from your child's school what is acceptable to use on campus, when, and where.

Likewise, if teachers provide an optional structure for specific playground activities, it may make the duration of time bearable for any number of kids, including those with Asperger's. As discussed, an alternative to being swallowed up by the lunchroom environment would be to establish "lunch bunch" discussion tables in a quieter corner of the cafeteria. Some schools assign seating on the bus, which helps quell anxiety in children with Asperger's, especially if seating is a daily "free for all" and the child must compete for seats with older children. One drawback to the concept of role assignment is that a child may become so rigid and unyielding that he is inflexible when it comes time to pass on the responsibility to another student. This should take place incrementally to transition the trade-off of responsibility wherever possible.

Important Points to Consider

You provide a positive environment for your child at home, but during the school year, much of his day is beyond your control. There are still things you can do to help your child deal with the pressures and stresses of a school day:

○ You know how your child learns best and what hindrances disrupt his learning. Communicate with your child's teacher so that she too is aware of the best ways to present information to your child.

○ Whenever possible, build on your child's strengths and passions, and encourage his teacher to do the same. Relate difficult assignments to things he is passionate about so that complex subjects become relatable.

○ Partner with your child's teacher (and aide). Together you all make up part of your child's team. Communicate honestly and openly with them as well as your child.

○ If your child demonstrates a need for perfection, let him know that no one is perfect and that it is okay to make mistakes. Share with him some mistakes you have made and encourage his teacher to do the same. When your child sees that even the adults in his life slip up, he may be less hard on himself.

○ Work with your child on constructing plans for unscheduled times of the school day (often slippery times for children with Asperger's). If your child is able to feel comfortable during these times, his school day will be less stressful and his learning less disrupted.

**CHAPTER 12**

Significant Transitions and Change

Because of your conscious focus on your child, you are probably already aware that change may be extremely difficult for her. Transitions of any kind, especially those that are unpredictable, can be unnerving and can cause your child to become totally undone. Being there to support your child through change is critical in order to make successful transitions. It is especially important in considering major childhood "life event" changes, such as attending a new school, moving, transition to college, divorce, or a death in the family.

Attending a New School

One of the mistakes parents and other adults make in interacting with children with Asperger's is in not preparing them for what's coming next. Changing jobs, having a new baby, or relocating to a new home are all exciting opportunities, but they are also stressful, overwhelming times. As an adult, you compensate for change by gathering as much information in detail as possible about who, what, when, where, why, and how. When you have incomplete information about future events, it heightens your anxiety in anticipation of the unknown. Too often, parents overlook sharing the same kinds of information with their child—information that would help her feel just as safe, comfortable, and in control of what's coming next.

It is likely there is little else in your child's perspective of her world as important—or anxiety-inducing—as school. If your child is a "pleaser," a perfectionist, socially challenged, or a stalwart rule-follower, school can seem like a life-or-death situation at times when things don't go as planned. The transition to a new school can include changing from elementary school to middle school or middle school to high school. It can also include moving to a new school district. No matter which of these situations your child is facing, she will rely upon you to guide her toward making predictable sense of it all. Give it as much attention and importance as it carries for her, but balance it with an air of fun and adventure. Remember, your child will reflect back to you what you project upon her. If your stress or anxiety shines through, it will directly affect the intensity of her anxiousness. Wherever possible, partner with your child in information gathering or, at the least, provide daily updates to quell her fears and butterflies. (She's probably already asking you the same questions repeatedly on a daily basis anyway.)

The word "change" in and of itself may be disconcerting for some children with Asperger's. Often, change is associated with loss of security and unpleasant circumstances. Instead, try discussing change from the perspective of opportunities to grow, learn, and mature—with your loving support and guidance.

Start by acknowledging that changing schools can be a scary or frustrating time because of so much being unknown. Moving up in grades is also a measure of growth and maturity. Reinforce with your child that she is growing and learning, and that she certainly wouldn't want to stay in her present grade level, even if it meant remaining in the same building. Pledge to support your child in demystifying as many of the unknowns as possible.

In addition, a school-team meeting should take place to plan for your child's transition, and, to ensure consistency, document the steps agreed upon. If the school does not offer such a meeting, contact your child's school to request that the principal schedule one. If you learn such a meeting cannot be held, request, in writing, to reopen your child's IEP for the purpose of including information in planning the transition. The focus of that portion of the meeting should be exclusively on supporting your child to transition to a new school with as much ease and comfort as possible. What follows are some strategies that should prove useful and might be discussed in detail at such a meeting.

PREPARATIONS

If possible, it will be most helpful for your child to meet next year's primary or homeroom teacher before the end of her current school year. In fact, in addition to meeting in person, it will probably be beneficial to arrange for that teacher to observe your child in class to glean firsthand information about her learning style, as well as to demystify Asperger's Syndrome in general. (Many teachers may not know much—if anything—about Asperger's Syndrome if they haven't had a student with Asperger's previously.)

It will also prove very helpful if your child's new teacher could "make himself real," so to speak, to your child in advance of meeting face-to-face. The concept of making oneself real can apply to anyone in your child's life, but it is particularly important with adults, especially those in caregiving roles. Adults in your child's life are the keepers of a lot of information about your child. This includes family history, medical history (including allergies and medications), psychological and psychiatric history, dietary background, educational records, and more. The balance of the scales of the relationship is tipped unevenly because your child has nowhere near a similar depth of information about the adults in her life as they do about her.

Many children with differences have a long parade of "cardboard cutouts" (in the outline of caregivers and educators) coming in and out of their lives without any personal investment in the relationship on the child's part. By demystifying the adults as human beings, the cardboard façades are shed and there is reason to begin to trust in the relationship. To begin, new teachers can provide your child with a clear, up-to-date photograph of themselves (a photograph in which someone has a different hair color and style, or facial hair where now they have none, will only be confusing and potentially upsetting). Attached to the photograph, teachers may add, in bullet-point sentences, any personal data each feels most comfortable sharing. Some examples include:

○ Full name, with an indication that the teacher is to be addressed only as Mr., Mrs., or Miss/Ms., unless special circumstances prevail

○ Birthday (note that it's *birthday* not *birth date*—no one should feel compelled to reveal their age) and birthstone

○ Favorite color(s)

○ Car make, model, color, and year (Some kids will love knowing how many miles are on your car, too!)

○ Favorite music

○ Hobbies and passions

○ Pets and their names

○ Loved ones and children

○ Favorite sports (as a participant or spectator)

○ Favorite places to vacation or visit

These are just a few examples to which many more may be added at each individual's discretion. The concept of "making yourself real" may also be adapted to aid all students in feeling comfortable with their teacher on the first day of school, and can even be used as an icebreaker among the entire class, if a teacher facilitates it. Similarities in likes, dislikes, and passions may emerge that could lend themselves to linking your child socially with others right from the first day of school. Other adults in your child's school career who may wish to consider participating in this process include:

- Principal
- Office secretaries
- Aides, therapists, or instructional assistants
- School bus or van drivers
- Custodians
- Cafeteria staff
- School nurse
- Librarians

One teacher started off the school year by requesting that all students create an "about me" collage of images designed to, at a glance, communicate their personalities, likes, and interests. He also participated and, at the end of the school year, gave his female student with Asperger's a notebook, the cover of which he had decorated with football images—his passion—in remembrance of him.

Equipped with personal information that deconstructs all these individuals as "real" people, your child may find herself with a greater level of comfort and confidence in approaching each individual as needed.

ADJUSTING TO THE SCHOOL ENVIRONMENT

Your child should also feel a sense of empowerment and ownership if provisions are made to familiarize her with the new school building. If you allow her to take the lead in this, all the better. You can do this by scheduling at least one visit to the new building and arming your child with a camera or camcorder to record the proceedings, allowing her to be in charge of directing the "movie" for the day. In this way, your child can independently quell her anxiety by reviewing the images as often as she wishes at her leisure and at home, where she feels safe and comfortable.

With each viewing, she should feel less anxious and more comfortable about the impending environment (she will have enough to deal with in getting acclimated as it is). Start by taking pictures or running a video beginning with the point at which she will be dropped off in front of the building; you'll want to ensure that everything will be replicated as close as possible in "real life" that first school day, but for now, it's a "dress rehearsal." Next, move inside the building and follow the path your child will take according to her schedule (which you and your child should have well in advance of the start of school). Obtaining a map of the property's layout for your child to keep should also prove useful. Specify all the rooms and exits your child may use, identifying each as you go. You know your child best, and, as she may be preoccupied with picture-taking, be certain to note any sensory-sensitivity triggers in the environment—smells, tastes, or visuals. This will help her to prepare and plan some subtle adaptations or accommodations.

Your child's locker assignment, or the place where her belongings will be stored, should also be captured on film. Additionally, the final product from the visit—pictures or videos—can be viewed with siblings and other family members with your child narrating the highlights (enhancing her personal investment and elevating comfort levels). The images can also be shared with her same-age friends who haven't had the benefit of the sneak preview of the new school environment.

Finally, be certain that your child has her own way of visually counting down the days until the transition by marking off a calendar or some other timekeeping device. Be prepared for her anxiousness to grow and be ready to offer reassurances, answer questions, or review the materials she already has in her possession (making yourself real pictures and stories, and visual images of the school building). Transitioning to a new school will be taxing and stressful for your child but, with these preparations in place, it should be much more manageable for her.

CONCERNS ABOUT BULLYING

If your child has anxiety about being identified as an easy target for abuse, find out about the new school's bullying policy and obtain it in writing to review and share with your child. Follow up with the administration if you have any questions or concerns about incident investigation or accountability. As previously noted, your child should know exactly whom she can tell about any incidents in which she has felt verbally or physically bullied.

Does the school provide a peer mentor or some other student who can show your child around in a discreet, nonstigmatizing way with the potential for friendship? How will you receive communication from the school about any issues that arise? Also, it will be helpful to aid your child's transition if she is well aware, in advance, of any responsibilities that can be assigned to her during unstructured activity times. Some schools offer structured indoor activities as alternatives to recess and other unstructured times.

Transition to New Home

If your child's school environment is a social jungle fraught with peril or inconsistency, then home is her fortress of sanctuary. Your child's house— and bedroom in particular—is home base, a safe, impenetrable island in which she can relinquish her masquerade of neurotypical "normalcy" and be herself by herself. You've experienced what can occur if you or anyone else disrupts this sanctuary without adequate notice. Now, imagine what it can mean for your child if the physical structure of her room (and, by extension, her entire home) is threatened or removed because your family is relocating to a new living environment. Your child may experience resistance, denial, and emotional upset when you break the news of the move to another house. Depending upon the reason for the move, it may be easier to accept some rationales than others (e.g., job transfer versus divorce). Be wary of your child's potential to dip into a depressed state at this time as well. In any case, it will be important to partner with your child in as many facets of this process as possible.

Once the initial shock and heartbreak of the news subsides (yes, it can be that traumatic), share with your child thoughts about all the impending unknowns that face you and your family. If your child is an oldest child, can she assist you in breaking the news to younger siblings, cousins, neighbors, or other family members? This kind of "adult" responsibility can empower your child to shift her perspective of the move to a more selfless position. Think of some of the other responsibilities you can share with her to make the move more palatable and less threatening. Perhaps she could:

- Scan the Internet to locate Realtors, new home listings, and other related information

- Help you to schedule dates and times to meet with Realtors to view prospective homes

- Help arrange showings of your current home

- Begin to inventory household and personal belongings

- Plan a garage sale or designate items for drop-off donation

- Start to prioritize packing and labeling moving boxes

- Identify all utility companies that require notification of the move

- Fill out change-of-address cards

- Determine data involving the geographic location of the move, mileage to and from the destination, and other pertinent logistics

When viewing potential new homes, allow your child to accompany you whenever possible. Encourage her to ask questions of the Realtor related to areas of interest or importance for her. This will help quell her anxieties, and you may be surprised to hear her ask questions you hadn't thought to ask yourself. As with transitioning to a new school, once you've narrowed your choices of location to a select few, plan to document the final decision-making visits by taking photos or videos. Not only will this be an aid to your child, it will be equally helpful to you for recalling certain details.

During these walk-throughs, give your child the chance to speculate with you about room designations, potential location of furniture,

There are no two ways about it: Moving to a new home, especially under duress or unpredictable circumstances (such as divorce or a death in the family), will have great impact on your child. Though this is likely a stressful and hectic time for everyone, make yourself available to listen to your child's (perhaps repeated) concerns. Illustrating or writing about the experience might be a helpful way of venting for her to process the anxiety.

changes in décor, and so on. If you are building a new home, it will be equally beneficial to you and your child to document the building process (with your child manning the camera). Moving day will still be very emotional for you all, but maintaining a positive attitude about a new beginning and a fresh start will be of immeasurable value.

Transition to College

Another major life change for young people is the prospect of attending college after high school graduation. If your child's diagnosis has been identified and supported in your school district, a transition plan to support your child from graduation to higher education, technical or training school, or employment of some sort should have been implemented by age fourteen with specific resources and contacts identified; a specific vocational plan should be in place by age sixteen. Your child may be eligible to continue attending school until age twenty-one, and it is not unusual for students with Asperger's to remain behind their graduating class.

Some high schools may offer a school-to-work transition program or may partner with local colleges to offer higher-education opportunities while your child is still attending high school. Inquire about such opportunities well in advance of your child's senior year of school; there may be a waiting list, limited availability, or sign-up procedures.

THE DECISION TO ATTEND COLLEGE

Even if your child's school experience hasn't always been a glowing one, it has offered some measure of life stability. With the advent of graduation, another transition is impending that can, again, create emotional upheaval. Hopefully, at some point in your child's school career, a psychologist or guidance counselor has completed an inventory of your child's aptitudes—strengths, gifts, and talents. While there likely won't be anything there that comes as a surprise to you, the results of such an assessment can provide a valuable starting point in weighing future vocational or educational paths for your child to pursue. Your child's school should also be able to assist you and her in matching her strengths and skills with schools known for their expertise in those select areas, such as the college with a strong science program or the university known for its music department. Literature and other resources can be obtained with the support of your child's guidance counselor or other staff. Encourage your child to make appointments to meet with this individual to gather information and tips on filling out applications. (If your child procrastinates for whatever reason, set deadlines by which you expect her to meet your expectations. Her internal sense of apprehension may be misinterpreted as laziness or lack of motivation.) Your child's school staff should be willing to support this endeavor through to completion. Again, the attitude of everyone around your child will be of immeasurable benefit in framing this time as a maturing "rite of passage" and not something to be filled with dread.

WHAT'S INVOLVED?

The word "college" has taken on numerous and varied connotations in recent times. This new flexibility is heartening to those children who have one perception of college as an "all or nothing" scenario; that is, some upset or resistance to college may come from the belief that college means packing up and leaving home, returning only at holidays and semester breaks. In partnership with your child, explore all that "going off to college" can mean, including:

O Attending college in another state (living on campus)

O Attending college in another part of your current state (living on campus)

- Working part-time and attending night classes (on campus or living at home)

- Starting out slowly by taking fewer classes (on campus or living at home)

- Starting out slowly by living at home but commuting to a local college

- Taking classes online over the Internet

- Taking correspondence courses

- Attending a branch campus before relocating to the main campus

- Considering how to transfer schools (and credits) if things aren't working out, or as part of a plan

As with transitioning to a new school building, you and your child will want to feel as fully prepared as possible well in advance of beginning school. This time, there will be far more details to keep track of. Ensure that you are maintaining the literature, directions, contacts and references, and campus maps as organized as possible, and keep notes cataloged well and in writing. As before, carefully photograph or videotape everything, marked clearly, to review as often as necessary in order to make a final decision or just familiarize your child with the surroundings.

The traditional unknowns include selection of roommates and scheduling classes. Take into account the location of classes and the time allotted between classes, in addition to the distance from your child's residence (or the parking lot, if commuting) to classes. Some kids, not as graceful or agile as they wish to be, may find it physically depleting to spend a lot of time walking long distances, especially in inclement weather. Conversely, if your child has too much time between classes, it can be socially awkward to find ways to fill such downtime, especially if he is a commuter. Liane Holliday Willey's book *Pretending to Be Normal* offers myriad suggestions to new college students for how best to assimilate on campus.

ONE PROGRAM THAT WORKS

The Center for Student Progress at Youngstown (Ohio) State University offers a model program of support to students with Asperger's Syndrome. On-site coordinators, who work from the center's office, meet weekly with identified students. Upon admission, any such student meets with a coordinator to whom she is assigned and completes a Participant Agreement that defines the obligation of the center as well as expectations of the student's participation in the program. By signing the Participant Agreement, the student also gives permission for a release of information so that test scores, grades, and other assessments are shared with her coordinator. It is an important function of the contract and allows the coordinator to access student grades and provide feedback early on in each semester so that any action needed to improve grades can be planned well in advance of failing a course.

Other aids provided to students with Asperger's by Youngstown State's Center for Student Progress include a Study Schedule that is filled out by each student and visually maps how to get organized, use time wisely, and plan when and where to devote time to studying. A calendar, again maintained by both parties, records test dates and assignment and project due dates. When a student comes in to meet with her coordinator, the coordinator can, at a glance, get a sense of where the student should be in her class management and can ask how she is progressing. Finally, a learning style inventory is a simple, easy-to-read questionnaire that helps the center's coordinators to determine the type of learning style unique to each student (visual learner, auditory learner, or kinesthetic learner—someone who learns best through moving and doing). Supporting the student to identify her learning style and adapt study habits to some helpful techniques is another of the coordinator's responsibilities. This may, in turn, lead to accommodations necessary to achieve success in certain classes, such as a professor's flexibility in how graded notebooks are submitted if your child reinforces certain concepts with illustrations.

There is also a checklist called Strategies for Reaching Goals that includes not only academic milestones desired but social objectives as well, such as joining a student organization, attending an athletic event, and participating in other on-campus social events. Many other activities may be involved, depending upon the individual needs of each student.

Your child's selection of higher-education institution may be influenced by the kinds of on-campus supports available to her. Check with each school under consideration to determine the scope and extent of support for students with Asperger's Syndrome. This may look very different from services available to students with disabilities, which include physical adaptations and accommodations.

The type and degree of available support similar to the Youngstown State University program may be a decision-making factor in your child's college selection. At the very least, making that single connection with someone who will function as an ally is crucial to your child's ability to assimilate successfully. But college is also about broadening one's social contacts. An ally may be gained informally, or the relationship may be prearranged through a student mentorship program on campus. Most forward-thinking, progressive universities have programs established to aid students with disabilities, but finding those that have expertise in the subtleties of Asperger's Syndrome may prove challenging.

Handling Divorce

Divorce is rarely an amicable situation. Occasional stress and tension in marriage is inevitable. The outward, vocal expression of arguments between married couples can vary from silent, passive-aggressive behavior to knock-down, drag-out, obscenity-shouting brawls. In any event, your very sensitive child with Asperger's Syndrome will probably sense marital discord long before you realize it yourself—even if you believe you've been very cautious. Parents, in the context of a loving and safe home environment, are the very rock of stability for all children, especially the child with Asperger's.

POTENTIAL REACTIONS

No child should have to grow up subjected to a tense, abusive home life in which parents interact in harsh and angry ways. The child with

Asperger's Syndrome may internalize what is transpiring around her and assume personal responsibility for it—even if none of the marital conflict is any reflection on her. It can be an utterly terrifying time, and the internal personalization of the situation cannot be contained indefinitely. In the child with Asperger's Syndrome, this can manifest itself in:

O Depressive symptoms

O Post-traumatic stress disorder

O Heightened anxiety

O Regular symptoms of physical illness

O Rashes, hives, and other skin irritations

O An increase in "acting out" or other attention-seeking behaviors

O Increased difficulty in school

Resolving the situation, maintaining peace wherever possible, and providing assurances as divorce is impending should aid the situation. Only you can determine if other interventions, such as psychiatric counseling, would be appropriate to augment your efforts. If so, you will need to ensure that such intervention is tailored to accommodate your child's way of understanding and interpreting information.

EXPLAINING DIVORCE

Most children are naturally inclined to believe that they are somehow the cause of a divorce. This may be intensified in your child with Asperger's and will be reinforced if she witnessed or overheard conflicts in which she was at the center of an argument. It is also natural for any child to feel emotional upheaval in wondering whom to "side" with, especially if one parent plays the child against the other. Even if you are seeking to escape a harmful or abusive situation, your child with Asperger's is likely to feel emotionally torn. In such a situation, all children will require constant assurances during a time in which uncertainty about the future reigns. This will be especially true of the child with Asperger's, and, as you've learned, verbal assurances are not enough.

Your approach to a mindful divorce is a dissolution of a formal spousal relationship through a contemplative assessment of the individual strengths and limitations of each party involved. Approaching this resolution with regard and concern will set an example of grace for your child with Asperger's.

Your child will require pictures, words, and stories to help make sense of it all and to foster some measure of safety and comfort. It will be helpful to make private time alone with your child. If you and your spouse are civil with one another, meeting together with your child will be an optimal demonstration of solidarity and goodwill. Explain the circumstances as you would to any of your children. Don't be surprised if your child with Asperger's punctuates your discussion with her own recollections of marital conflicts that stretch back in time—some of which you may have forgotten or of which you failed to realize the full impact. Encouraging your child to write, draw, cartoon storyboard, or use the computer to communicate her feelings and understanding of the situation should be helpful. Review and fine-tune this information with her regularly and be prepared to follow her lead in opening up discussion at times you hadn't anticipated it. Sights, sounds, and smells can trigger thoughts that will lead to your child's need to verbalize her feelings.

Your child may well have to decide where and with whom she'd like to live. This can snowball and lead to other social upheavals concerning a new home, new neighborhood, new family members, and a new school. It may also mean leaving behind friends, family, pets, and familiar environments.

It is important to stress and review all the things that will stay the same during this transition in addition to walking through the future changes, and to do so often throughout the process (foremost of which should be your unconditional love). Be clear in communicating that the divorce is not your child's fault and demystify any new environmental changes in ways similar to those described in transitioning to a new school.

Loss of Loved Ones

The loss of a loved one can never be fully anticipated. Consider the range of emotions you may experience, such as grief, guilt, shock, loneliness, compassion, and humor, and think of how that might reflect in your child with Asperger's Syndrome. The difference may be that while you and others close to you may outwardly show such emotions, you may not readily detect such feelings in your child. Just like you, comprehending the loss of a loved one (even a beloved pet) may take time for your child to completely process. Because your child isn't grieving in "typical" ways, such as openly sobbing or wanting to be with and talk to close family or friends, doesn't mean she isn't experiencing everything you are. The opposite could, in fact, be true.

EXPLAINING DEATH

Remember that honesty is the best policy. You may be pressured by well-meaning friends or relatives to offer some alternate explanation for the loss of a loved one, such as "Uncle Rich has gone away and won't be back," "Daddy's just sleeping," "Your baby sister won't be coming home from the hospital," or "Grandma's resting in the ground now." At some point your white "fib" will be exposed and the cover-up—despite your original best intentions—could upset the trust between you and your child.

In explaining death, you will wish to call upon your own religious and spiritual beliefs as the foundation from which to begin such a discussion with your child. Analogies, such as referring to other people who have passed or transition metaphors like the butterfly, may be helpful—as will drawing and writing out what you intend to communicate and reviewing it regularly.

FOLLOW-UP SUPPORT

Follow your child's lead. It is not helpful to exclude your child from participating in any of the subsequent formalities attendant to funerals or other rituals if she expresses her desire to partake (although an open-casket situation can be visually confusing and distressing for many). In fact, if you can in some small way assign your child a responsibility, it may help her to maintain focus amid what may be a chaotic and upsetting time. This may be especially helpful for the preadolescent or teen.

Don't become angered if your child catches you off-guard with seemingly insensitive questions about the mechanics of embalming, cremation, burial, and the like. These are honest inquiries designed to contribute to your child's understanding and comfort level; answer them just as honestly, or explain your discomfort with discussing those subjects at present but refer your child to others who might be willing to do so, or perhaps look up similar, generic information on the Internet. Also, at this time don't be quick to scold if your child's emotions aren't considered appropriate to the moment, such as laughing during a solemn discussion—she may be on emotional burnout and distracting herself by playing a mind movie. Finally, don't be surprised, dismiss it as imagination, or blatantly disregard it if your child reports that she has seen, talked with, smelled, or otherwise interacted with the loved one who has recently passed. Remember that your child may be very sensitive to many things, seen and unseen. Instead, validate what your child tells you by listening carefully, requesting further information, asking clarifying questions, providing assurances, and reinforcing her communication wherever possible.

Important Points to Consider

Change can be difficult for all children but especially for those with Asperger's Syndrome. You will need to be there to support your child and be open to her questions and concerns no matter what they might be. Remember that children with Asperger's often view things in a much more concrete way than others of the same age and so they might have more trouble adjusting to change. Whether the change is a new school, new living conditions, or the loss of a loved one, be understanding of your child's unique needs. Here are some things to consider:

○ Prepare your child for change as much as possible. If she is changing to a new school, let her visit the new school well in advance of the change. If the change is a new home, allow her to be part of the home selection process and listen to her opinions.

○ Include your child in decisions about the change whenever possible. Make her feel like a key player.

○ Help your child meet as many people as possible who will be part of the new situation. Doing so will help your child's comfort level and help her build more "allies."

○ For unforeseen or sudden changes such as death, be open and honest with your child. She may have unsettling questions, but this is often how children with Asperger's deal with change—by amassing as much knowledge about the situations as they can. Answer your child as truthfully as possible and resist the urge to sugarcoat things.

○ Help your child find avenues to express her feelings about the change. Drawing, journaling, or talking with a trusted person could all be methods to help your child.

○ Remember, verbal reassurances will not be enough for your child with Asperger's. You need to find ways to *show* her that the change will be okay.

CHAPTER 13

Sexuality

Many people are uncomfortable discussing issues of sexuality, but since you've been open and honest with your child in other matters, this subject should be no different. Supporting your child as a person with Asperger's Syndrome means supporting the whole person, including sexuality. Some parents prefer not to "go there" in their thinking and struggle with perceiving their child as a budding adult. However, if you stay attuned to your child's growing needs as he ages and matures, you will be a resource to him concerning issues of sexuality.

The Birds and the Bees

As with any of your children, you will want to discuss with your spouse, in advance, how best to explain issues of a sexual nature to your child with Asperger's. Many children broach the topic first—a cue for parents to guide them into such discussions. For example, your child may enjoy watching animal or nature-related programs on TV, or you may own pets that deliver litters of puppies, kittens, or hamsters. Inevitably, your child will be exposed to the facts of life via images of animals mating with one another, and this may prompt questions about reproduction or sexual attraction. Your child may have also intruded upon your own lovemaking unexpectedly; this requires prompt explanation as well for purposes of damage control.

Understand that for all children, observation of sexual acts can be grossly misinterpreted. Facial expressions, vocalizations, and body position can make the scenario appear violent and hurtful, and anything but passionate. The child with Asperger's—witnessing such activity without explanation—may burn this image into his brain and associate it exclusively with sexual activity, setting an unpleasant precedent. Shouting in alarm at your child upon discovery will only reinforce such negative thoughts and feelings.

Many people with differences have been taught that it is inappropriate to have sexual thoughts, feelings, or indulgences at all. One young adult with Asperger's has been so brainwashed that he harms himself whenever he has sexual thoughts in order to exact punishment for thinking "dirty" things. As a parent, you may see your son or daughter as a perpetual child because of a childlike naiveté about so many aspects of life and socialization. The truth is, we are all sexual beings, even children. Attempting to control or suppress someone's sexuality is akin to assuming authority over that person's humanity. No one has the right to assume such an audacious position over another person, whether that person experiences a different way of being or not.

The best way to enter into what will be a series of ongoing discussions with your child about sex is to be open and honest, using clear language paired with visuals. There are a number of well-illustrated books available that explain animal and human reproduction, including pop-up books, which might be helpful. Videos may also be available at your library or on *www.youtube.com*.

APPROACHING THE SUBJECT

Your comfort level with your own sexuality will determine how effective you are. Presenting material in a "hit or miss" manner (e.g., being out of the room while your child absorbs the information alone) may create more confusion and send a message that you are unapproachable. Be available to your child during and after such dialogues so that you can quickly clarify anything that might be upsetting or cause for concern.

Quickly dispel any rumors or myths your child may bring home. Your child may hear wildly imaginative and completely false stories about what happens during the act of sex, which is scary stuff that can fuel anxieties about an already confusing process. When discussing sexual organs, avoid using cutesy or slang terms—there is great potential for your child to associate those words with certain body parts exclusively for some time to come, making the introduction of the proper words confusing.

> Human sexuality can be a complex matter. Just like everyone else, people with Asperger's Syndrome have identified their sexuality as heterosexual, homosexual, or bisexual. Still others communicate a disinterest or lack of desire to engage in a romantic or sexual relationship with any partner. Please be prepared to be sensitive and respectful of your child's individual sexuality.

Again, follow your child's lead about the type and degree of information to share, paired with visuals. To alleviate any misunderstanding that sex is a physical act for the sake of sex alone, ensure that the discussion occurs within the context of love—a concept that may be challenging for some children who, at a tender age, associate love exclusively with parents, friends, and family. This will help quell any fears about sexual acts being hurtful or repressive. Explain that, because of feeling euphoric in the moment, sex may look and sound like something it's not. It is important to emphasize that while you are always willing and accessible to discuss sexual matters, it is a private matter that should not be discussed publicly, especially within earshot of others. List, in writing, the places and times that it is okay to discuss sex, such as when you are alone with your child in the car or at home watching something on TV that provokes his curiosity.

GROWING UP

You will wish to periodically revisit these conversations as your child matures, if he or she doesn't broach the subject first. Most significantly, be prepared to discuss sexuality at the onset of your child's adolescence. A changing, maturing body, complete with growing pains, sprouting body hair, or menstruation, can be another very frightening time if not handled carefully, well in advance and framed in a very positive light.

As your child grows, you may discover her sexuality beginning to flourish. Be certain to counsel her privately to quickly curb any overtly sexual remarks or similar flirtatious self-expressions to support her in avoiding social embarrassment. Others may completely misinterpret her communications and label them in stigmatizing ways. If necessary, dig out your old list of when, where, and with whom it is okay to talk about sex. Or compose a new list. At a certain age, it may not be "cool" to continue having these discussions with one's parent, so, while you will always wish to be accessible, the list may be expanded to include a circle of safe and trusted friends who can be relied upon to keep your son or daughter's confidence and give accurate feedback.

Masturbation

Remember that many individuals with Asperger's have a strong associative connection when learning new concepts or social "rules." If you send your child the message that masturbation is unequivocally wrong or perpetuate antiquated myths about going blind or growing hairy hands, he will believe it, and such notions will imprint upon your child a disturbing, harmful view of acting upon one's sexual thoughts through masturbation.

For many, masturbation is one of the few forms of pleasurable release that can be individually controlled. The essential concept to communicate here is one of public versus private masturbation. If you are unsure or uncomfortable about broaching the subject of masturbation, here is a sample story used to introduce the basics to a preadolescent boy. The strategy is that he reads it with a trusted ally (you, if that applies) and afterward has a forum in which to ask questions. The story should become his personal property, and he may review the "rules" about masturbation at his leisure. You can adapt the same story to meet the needs of your daughter.

My body is my own. My body is beautiful. My body is made up of many different parts, inside and out. Inside parts are like my heart and stomach. Outside parts are like my arms and legs. The outside parts that are between my legs and covered by my underwear are called my sexual organs. My sexual organs are my penis and my testicles. Many boys and men touch, rub, or gently pull their penis. When this happens, their penis usually gets bigger and harder. The same thing may happen to me. This is normal and okay. If I touch, rub, or gently pull my penis, this is called masturbation. Many boys and men masturbate. Masturbation is a choice that is my own to make.

If I choose to masturbate it may be because I am thinking about sex. It may be because I am thinking about another person. It may be because I want to feel good. It may be because I want some time alone with my body. It may be for other reasons.

When I masturbate, I may feel excited inside. I may breathe harder. I may breathe faster. This is normal and okay. When I masturbate, I may get so excited that my penis ejaculates. This means that something white and wet comes out of the opening in the tip of my penis. It is called semen or sperm. I may not ejaculate semen or sperm every time I masturbate. But if I do, this is normal and okay.

If I choose to masturbate, I will try to remember to masturbate in a private place. This means I will go to a place where there are no other people around. This means I will go to a place where I can be alone with my body. A private place may be my bedroom or a bathroom.

People masturbate in a private place because sexual organs are private. People wear underwear and clothes to keep their sexual organs private. People expect one another to masturbate in a private place. People will also expect me to masturbate in a private place. It is like a rule. A place that is not private is a place with other people around me. If I touch my sexual organs when I'm in a place that is not private—even if I'm wearing pants—people may be upset. They may laugh at me. They may be angry. They may report me to the police. They may not think I am smart. They may think these things because people expect one another to masturbate in a private place. If I masturbate in a place that is not private, I am breaking a rule that people expect me to know.

I will try not to touch my sexual organs, or put my hands in my pants, or masturbate in a place that is not private. I will try to remember to masturbate only in a private place. Masturbation is a choice that is my own to make. It is normal and okay.

Infatuation

As your child with Asperger's blossoms into a teenager, he is also developing as a sexual young adult. He may be finding himself sexually attracted to others more and more, and perhaps is finding a social niche by imitating the way he sees others interacting. He may develop crushes typical of any young person feeling a strong connection with another because of mutual interests, compatible personalities, or similar skills and talents.

Some stalkers of high-profile celebrities may also fit an Asperger's Syndrome profile, in addition to being deemed mentally ill. Their personal, unconventional logic, intrinsic backgrounds, and antisocial activities have been cited as contributors to their obsessive drive. Your challenge is to keep communication channels open with your child in navigating and balancing teen and young-adult romance to avoid unfair mislabeling.

IS IT LOVE?

Like anyone, some young people with Asperger's can grossly misjudge the depth or reciprocation of potentially romantic relationships with others. This may be an extremely confusing time for your child. Much of what is considered sexual chemistry between two people is unspoken, subtle, or steeped in innuendo—including all facial-expression and body-language cues your child may have difficulty tapping into. Because many people with Asperger's think of social behavior in clear-cut terms, your child may overestimate the intent of the other party in the relationship. (In the cruelest of circumstances, the other person may be "playing" your child, setting him up to fall for his or her own amusement; or the person may have been put up to it by others with similarly disingenuous motives.) It may also be that the other person only perceives your child as just a friend.

UNREQUITED CRUSH

The challenge is that some kids with Asperger's don't recognize the nuances of what's friendship and what's puppy love (or full-blown, young-adult romance). In some instances, this misinterpretation can lead the individual with Asperger's, perhaps driven by genuine affection, to become intensely infatuated. This may demonstrate itself through symptoms similar to those of obsessive-compulsive disorder—not eating or sleeping regularly, inability to focus and concentrate, thinking about nothing but the other person. Be especially watchful for symptoms of depression at this time as well.

If your child is misinterpreting social cues, is in denial or disbelieving of another's communications, or won't take "no" for an answer, there is potential for him to be accused of stalking or harassment, especially if this is the first time he's experienced such intense feelings of affection. On occasion, a person may go to extremes to make his plea known, such as harming himself or threatening to kill the person, taking radical measures in a public environment such as school, or other similar threats. Usually, these are nothing more than cries for attention (you know your child to be a gentle, quiet individual), but, in this day and age, severe communications of this nature are not tolerated and schools are quick to enforce serious consequences in reaction to such threats. Any pronouncement of the intent to harm oneself or others, or attempts to do so, must be treated very seriously with swift intervention.

At this time, it will be wise to gauge, day by day, your child's activities; most of these (including the interactions he enjoys) will occur away from home, during the day, and in school. Ensure that you are regularly asking specific, detailed questions about his day, particularly if you suspect something is wrong.

> Having balance in one's life can be of immeasurable aid in how people approach challenges. If your child has meaningful responsibilities, unconditional allies, and opportunities to explore passions, coping with relationship obstacles may be less likely to become an all-consuming focus.

There is also the flip side to consider. In one instance, a boy with Asperger's misinterpreted the romantic advances of a girl, thinking they were just friends. Apparently she became so impatient and frustrated at his lack of sexual savvy that she stood him up at a school dance. When she finally arrived, she acted cold and indifferent toward him, propelling him further into confusion. Hopefully, with your awareness and early guidance, your child will experience both successful and bittersweet (but manageable) romantic interactions.

Dating

When any two people meet and develop a gratifying romantic and sexual relationship, it often stems from a mutual vocation, avocation, or educational pursuit. Remember, passions are icebreakers in conversation and are relationship-builders as well. Building upon one's most passionate interests can lead directly to interacting with others similarly impassioned. Still, some people are drawn to each other because they compensate for each other's differences, strengths, and deficits. However two people are drawn together, new relationships of this nature can be difficult for anyone to navigate, and this is no different for your child with Asperger's.

Advancing a relationship can be an art form. Explain to your child that it's never wrong to simply ask the other person to be honest about what he or she is thinking and feeling. This is the only way many people with Asperger's will know definitively how to pursue the relationship. Any discussion about dating should also include an explanation of the potential for rejection by the other person. It is a trial-and-error, touch-and-go process for anyone. Be prepared to counsel your child in ways that are private and gentle; he has the potential to take rejection hard.

> There are a growing number of books about Asperger's Syndrome and relationships. Many of these volumes are personal accounts written by individuals with Asperger's themselves ("Aspies," as some affectionately call themselves). See Appendix A for a list of books on this subject.

Barney, an adult with Asperger's, shares an anecdote from his adolescence with amusement for the purpose of illuminating others about misunderstanding social customs. When he was in high school, "cruising" in cars up and down a main strip was popular. Boys in cars would shout out introductions to carfuls of girls. Barney, however, felt this was an inefficient way of communicating, since it required shouting over other cruisers. He constructed a small transmitter that allowed him to pick up on the radio signals that girls in a particular car were listening to. He would tune the transmitter to the radio of a carful of girls he was interested in, then pick up his microphone and speak to them "privately" through their radio. He would tune his transmitter, then, interrupting the music playing in their cars, he would describe the car they were driving and the clothes they were wearing. The girls would shriek and change radio stations, which Barney took to be part of a game of "playing hard to get." But he soon realized this wasn't the case, as they screamed at him to get out of their radios, and he received similar reactions from other carfuls of girls.

Mark Sachnik, a man with ASD who was a strong self-advocate, shared some thoughts about dating and evolving sexual relationships.

> Unfortunately, the "dating game" is probably one of the biggest challenges teenagers or young adults face in the process of growing up. Add autism (or any disability) into the mix and you could have

a recipe for disaster because these individuals will feel less and less comfortable with themselves. This is where it is extremely important for those around them to help them become more comfortable with themselves and to emphasize the importance of "being yourself." Accepting who you are and being yourself greatly increases your chances for a successful relationship, while nonacceptance and trying to "reinvent" yourself only increases your chances of failure.

Now for the really hard part. The individual with autism has met an "ideal mate," a common bond is established, and a really good friendship is "in the works." The individual is starting to develop feelings for the person. Again, there is absolutely nothing wrong with that. The problem individuals with autism run into is they will often have "no clue" on how to read "hints," tones of voice, or subtle "body language." It is very hard for them to decipher between romantic overtures and acts of friendship. This is when "social stories," complete with pictures (not the "graphic" kind) would really help.

A developing close relationship with a member of the opposite sex usually leads to thoughts of entering into a sexual relationship. Re-emphasize the facts of life and also reinforce the concept that a sexual relationship carries a lot of responsibility. This is also the time to discuss the possible consequences of entering into an irresponsible sexual relationship (a commitment before you are ready, unwanted pregnancy, sexually transmitted disease, etc.).

Same-Sex Attraction

Just as the causes of Asperger's are unknown, so are the causes of homosexuality—both are naturally occurring, and neither may be blamed as anyone's "fault." Society is making slow but positive strides in its growing acceptance of people with same-sex orientation, but there remain those who vehemently oppose and condemn any expression of homosexuality.

As a person identified with Asperger's Syndrome, your child is not the child you envisioned when he was first born. Having a same-sex orientation adds another layer to the circumstances that may be challenging for you to absorb as a parent. But as challenging as it may be for you, imagine how homosexuality may further complicate your child's life. Your child's self-image and self-esteem start with the feedback you provide as a parent. Your child is a person first and foremost—a magnificent, gorgeous, talented human being with so much to offer the world merely by being in it. Just as he is not defined exclusively by Asperger's Syndrome, he (and you) should not accept his being defined exclusively by a label of same-sex orientation.

As your child matures through adolescence, be mindful that a same-sex attraction may be a possibility and, like it or not, be prepared to embrace your child regardless. If your child's knowledge of his same-sex orientation is emerging at this time, he will be more vulnerable than ever before and need your unconditional love and acceptance to weather any storms ahead. An exception is the young child who, seeing something on television, becomes very concerned that he or she is gay even when, deep down, he or she knows it doesn't apply to him or her. This is a different situation than same-sex attraction.

In recent times, persons who identify as transgender are publicly advocating for themselves and others who experience Gender Identity Disorder. A February 2012 study published in the *Journal of Autism and Developmental Disorders* found that female-to-male transsexual people (those who are masculinized) had a higher probability of possessing autistic traits when compared with typical males and females and transwomen. The study concluded that transmen may have had difficulty socializing with female peers and identified more readily with male peers. Other studies have found potential associations with transgenderism and autistic traits. If you suspect your child may experience confusion about his or her gender identity, consult your pediatrician for information on how best to address it.

Internet groups are being established for people with Asperger's Syndrome who are gay, lesbian, bisexual, transgendered, or questioning. Parents, supportive partners, and family and friends are welcome to participate as well. Members who join GRASP, an Asperger's organization (*www.grasp.org*), may also access such an online group.

If you are unknowledgeable or uncertain about how to handle your child's same-sex orientation, find out what local resources are available—whom to call, what to research on the Internet, or what literature to obtain. Your positive, proactive support of your child will be helpful to him or her, tempered with a dialogue about privacy and discretion about one's sexual orientation—not out of shame but out of respect for others and oneself.

If you are a reasonably sophisticated, mature human being, you probably know, love, and accept any number of friends, family, and coworkers with a same-sex orientation. One mother acknowledged that her son with Asperger's was enduring tough times socially and emotionally but that his crowd of gay friends provided him a source of invaluable support. Another young man wants nothing more than to find a loving partner but slips further and further into a severely depressed state. Which scenario would you wish for your child? Dating is confusing and awkward for anyone of any age, so remember that your child with Asperger's needs as much support as you can give him during these years.

Important Points to Consider

Dating and sexuality are often difficult areas for parents to discuss with their children. Being there for your child, giving him advice, and supporting his decisions are all things you can do to help him wade through the rough waters of sexual issues. Here are some things to keep in mind:

O Children with Asperger's often have trouble deciphering social cues. Talk with your child and try to give him advice about how to read common situations.

O Be direct and honest when you talk to your child about sex. Children with Asperger's may become confused if you use cute names or innuendoes for describing body parts or acts. Use age-appropriate language and discuss age-appropriate issues.

O Your child may have a hard time understanding social cues in the world of dating. You can help by reading books or watching movies together that show reliable social situations, or even by sharing your own dating stories with him.

O Encourage honesty from your child in discussing sexual issues and be honest with your child in return. You can best support your child by forming a relationship in which he knows he can discuss even difficult issues with you.

 **CHAPTER 14**

Strategies of Lifelong Value

The greatest gift you can give your child with Asperger's Syndrome is a full awareness of self—her needs as well as her strengths—in order for her to become a self-advocate. It is important that your child have a "bag of tricks," an arsenal of strategies to employ that will be universally received as socially acceptable as she moves into adulthood.

Personal Schedules

One of the single greatest causes of heightened anxiety in children with Asperger's Syndrome is worrying about the future, that is, not knowing what's coming next. Maintaining control is crucial to kids with Asperger's, and they may become quickly and easily unhinged when routines change without warning or others are privy to information that isn't shared with them or isn't communicated until the last minute. As a result, too many kids with Asperger's are medicated with anxiety-reducing drugs. This is intervention, not prevention. Before such medicine is prescribed, consider implementing any number of the recommendations in this chapter, foremost being the personal schedule.

Almost all people have some sort of long-term date-keeping device, be it a mobile device, a calendar (perhaps on your computer desktop or iPhone), or a hard-copy date book in which you can manually plan for a day, week, or month at a time. Have you ever misplaced your date-keeping device? If so, perhaps you can begin to appreciate the kind of nervous anxiety experienced by those who are at the mercy of others to stay informed of what's upcoming. The longer you go without having your schedule—and knowing you are still responsible for keeping to it—the more upset and distressed you're likely to become. Many people joke that they couldn't function without their schedule and are totally at a loss without it. Why should your child be without a similar way of tracking time and independently assessing impending events and activities? It makes more sense to quell anxiety and foster independent resilience in your child by helping her create a personal schedule.

The advantages to supporting your child in initiating a personal schedule are as varied as they are for any person. A visual daily schedule keeps your child focused and oriented with respect to time, sequence of events, priorities, and knowledge of what's coming next.

HOW TO SCHEDULE

Here's how it works: If your child enjoys computers and other electronic equipment, go with her to select a mobile device to suit her needs and interests. If your child handwrites legibly enough for her to read her own writing—and she doesn't mind handwriting—then she may choose to use a hard-copy date book, like a daily, weekly, or monthly planner (available at any office supply store and an inexpensive alternative to a piece of technology). In any event, your child should select what appeals to her most, within your budget.

Wherever possible, in partnership with your child, set up the schedule for the next day the night before. Some parents already spend time tucking their child into bed and, at this time, orally review the next day; this concept simply builds upon that good and thoughtful discussion by making it tangible and concrete. Knowing what tomorrow is supposed to "look like" the night before, and having it all recorded so there's no forgetting or mistaking it, enables many kids with Asperger's to relax and sleep through the night.

WHAT TO SCHEDULE

The times when the schedule will come in most handy are during those large, unscheduled, unstructured blocks of time such as evenings, weekends, holidays, and summer vacation. It will be best to arrange the schedule in a specific sequence if possible. Try setting it up like a "To Do" list to visually identify what needs to get done and what has been accomplished. Start by scheduling one or two "preferred" activities (these may derive from your child's passions or interests) before scheduling a "nonpreferred" activity, such as a household chore or homework. Continue in this sequence—preferred/nonpreferred/preferred—as much as possible. In this way, there is an incentive to use the schedule; there is a sense of accomplishment in visually observing one's achievements; and the schedule isn't perceived as a punitive device used by you to control or manipulate. Fade out your involvement as soon as possible in favor of your child having authority over making the schedule, within parental parameters, of course. The schedule may also be used to indicate birthdays, anniversaries, special events, and appointments of all kinds.

When your child begins to "bug" you with repeated questions, or if she protests or procrastinates about a nonpreferred activity, simply refer back to the schedule—it's all there in black and white. You may suggest, "Well, what does your schedule say is next?" Many such confrontations between parent and child can be nipped in the bud because the child will realize that you can't argue with what's concrete (this doesn't negate occasional parental leniency, as you'd grant any child).

It's probably best not to schedule activities by specific times, unless your child wishes to do so, or you've agreed that Saturday night she can stay up an hour later, for example. Your child may be the type to become exasperated if the schedule isn't maintained to the minute. However, most children with Asperger's find it a very useful tool for feeling safe and comfortable and in control of knowing what's coming next.

The Touchstone

Many people with Asperger's (and autism) soothe themselves by repeatedly manipulating an object such as a straw, a piece of string, or some beads. They find comfort in the sameness of repeating the motion over and over, relishing the calm that the texture of the object in their hand brings. Self-soothing is a strength that should not be misinterpreted or mislabeled. It is used to maintain control, and you'll likely see it intensify when your child is on the verge of losing control, as when she's very happy or excited or angry and upset. It may also kick into high gear if your child is in an environment that is assaulting her senses. You do this too—it just looks a little different, such as nervously shaking your leg while seated or persistently chewing on a pen or the inside of your cheek when stressed.

Because we are all more alike than different, most of us carry with us a small object that soothes and quells us if we stop to focus on it. Such personal "touchstones" may include a wedding band or favored piece of jewelry, rosary beads or a cross, good luck charms, or photos of loved ones. We carry these objects with us for sentimental reasons or because they hold some significance. You may wish to consider offering your child a similar touchstone that will be of lifelong value. The difference here is that of discretion, meaning use of the object is secret and private, not public (which may be stigmatizing). The goal here is that the touchstone should remain unseen, such as in a pocket or worn around the neck, under clothing.

The next time you're feeling especially anxious or distressed, try stopping in the moment to assess your outward expression of those feelings. In the midst of this "mindful moment," you may find yourself unconsciously toying with a ring, a necklace, your hair, or some other device that provides a comforting diversion. This is not unlike the touchstone concept.

CHOOSING AN OBJECT

To begin, ask your child to select a viable touchstone. It will probably be something related to her passion(s), or it might be an object associated with someone with whom she shares a strong, loving bond, such as a grandparent. Advise your child, using words and visuals, that when she is feeling an extreme emotion—but is still in control—she need only touch the object through her clothing, or reach inside a pocket to hold it, and conjure up all that it means to her in the moment. You may use the following story to introduce the concept and modify it to suit your needs:

> People like objects that make them feel comfortable and happy. My (mom/dad/caregiver) uses a _____ in this way. People like to be reminded of other people or things that make them feel happy. Sometimes, I like to think about _____ (the reason for the touchstone). It reminds me of how happy I feel when I _____ (engage in the passion).
>
> I can't always _____ (do one's passion), especially when I'm away from home. I can carry _____ (the touchstone) in my pocket to remind me of good times. When I feel anxious or upset, I can touch or hold _____ (the touchstone) to help me think about _____ (the passion) and how happy it makes me feel. It's okay to feel anxious or upset. Everybody feels this way sometimes. By holding _____ (the touchstone), I may not feel as anxious or upset.

One young teenager with Asperger's beautifully demonstrated his understanding that the touchstone is discreet. During a counseling session, he showed his support team the orange odometer needle he had selected. But afterward, he privately approached his counselor to share his other touchstone: a figurine from the *Powerpuff Girls* cartoon. He recognized the need to keep the figurine out of sight and to be selective in showing it to others.

The Social Out

Too many children with Asperger's are able to keep composure all day long at school but then come home and release their pent-up frustration and anxiety in ways that stun parents and perplex educators who don't notice any difficulties at all during the school day. Most people regulate their time by interspersing it with breaks, little rewards, and other forms of downtime. These include chatting on the phone or texting, surfing the Internet, using the bathroom, getting a drink or snack, breaking to listen to the radio or watch TV, and other mini-indulgences. Because your child is extremely sensitive, she needs to learn how to pace herself during the day in similar ways in order to avoid becoming so saturated and overwhelmed that she melts down completely upon returning home.

There are very few social situations and environments that you can't extricate yourself from if you so choose. You can even decide to discontinue a dental exam and walk out if you wish. The child with Asperger's Syndrome may not recognize that any other option is available other than to remain in the situation—even if it is a situation that is making her feel anxious, upset, and distressed. When it escalates to the point of no return, the child may have a meltdown, shut down, and become unresponsive. Your child does have an option to avert public embarrassment and stigmatization through using the "social out."

EMPOWER YOUR CHILD

You can go anywhere in the United States and in virtually any situation use the words "Please excuse me," get up, and walk out and have that communication received in a socially acceptable manner. Your child has the right to be empowered with the same understanding, especially in school where the setting is "governed" by adults adhering to a rigid schedule. Many kids with Asperger's independently figure out how to get their needs met in a similar way; they just do it by going to the water fountain or taking frequent trips to the bathroom. The child who often disappears into the bathroom doesn't have an overactive bladder—he's intelligent enough to have surmised that it's one of the limited opportunities he has to find a relatively calm and quiet place where he can quell anxieties and regroup before going back out into battle.

In collaboration with your child's educational team, teach him to use the words "Please excuse me" or "Excuse me, I need a break." (This will require practice and reminders at first until he gets the hang of it.) It also needs to be understood that his communication will be honored with immediacy (this includes you, the parent, while in environments outside the home). If your child's communication of the social out is not honored with immediacy but instead with vague statements like, "Hang in there a little bit longer," or "We'll go soon," you've disempowered him and taught him that he really has no control and that, ultimately, adults retain all the control and don't listen.

USING THE SOCIAL OUT

Interpret your child's social out as a strength. What he is really communicating is, "I've held it together for as long as I can, and if we don't get out of here now, it's going to get ugly." It is a mark of self-awareness of one's own experience in the moment. It is not about escaping responsibility; don't see it as manipulation.

There are very few situations in which you are compelled to remain from start to finish. Reflect on the number of times throughout a typical day that you routinely excuse yourself from social settings to address your personal needs. You may be surprised by the frequency.

Once they catch their breath and can process what was happening, most kids will be okay to return to the environment (unless it was overly stimulating). It may appear that your child is abusing the social out at first; he's not—your trust is being tested to see if you really will honor it every time. This should fade away as a mutual trust is recognized, but, if not, you might wish to assess your child's environment or the expectations placed upon him in the environment so that adaptations and accommodations may be made.

Acting and Music

Many young people with Asperger's absolutely flourish when given the opportunity to become involved in theater and acting. Many children with Asperger's are naturally brilliant actors and adept mimics, known to entertain others with their dead-on impersonations of TV and cartoon characters. Why not build upon this talent? There is so much to acting that holds special appeal for certain kids:

O You get to become someone other than who you are, which is attractive particularly if you have damaged self-esteem.

O You never say the wrong thing because everything you need to say is already scripted for you.

O If you are challenged in deciphering facial expressions and body language, you get a perfectly acceptable chance to practice understanding such nuances over and over again—it's called rehearsal.

O You are collaborating with others to produce a work of quality.

O There are social connections to be had with others who may be intrigued with or more accepting of others' differences.

O If you're good at what you do, you get positive feedback from your peers or an audience (through applause).

A lot of young people with Asperger's already act every day through using "movie talk." Movie talk (or TV talk) is a skill by which the person has artfully "lifted" lines of dialogue, facial expressions, and even body language from characters in favorite movies, television programs, or cartoon shows and "put it back out" with uncanny accuracy and with all the proper inflections. Many adults with Asperger's have "passed" in life by using movie talk to blend in fairly seamlessly. It is not something to discourage in your child but should be used to facilitate social interactions. The key is not to become the fictional character but to assume that character's most socially acceptable traits and make them your own until you feel more comfortable in your own skin. Some folks use movie talk to break the ice in conversation or to initiate an interaction using humor.

You probably recognized early on in your child's development how listening to her music—favorite songs and melodies—was extremely important. Like acting, all of music is scripted as well. Music therapists know the terms "call" and "response" as they apply to the flow of music. In reading, singing, or playing music, there is a time when one is an active participant in the "conversation." At this time, according to the script, you make your contribution to the song, whether it is through singing or playing an instrument. That's the call. The response comes when, according to the script, you are expected to remain silent and await the reply from one's communication partner(s). Your child may be absolutely passionate about music and performing music. You can use the concept of how music "works" as an analogy for how social conversation is supposed to flow.

Written Narratives

The concept of writing stories to aid students to understand social situations and peer conversation was pioneered by a woman named Carol Gray, who is a special education instructor working with kids with different ways of being. She discovered that her students who were especially visual learners had difficulty retaining verbal information and applying it in the context of social settings that would be obvious to most others. For example, one young man didn't understand the concept of raising his hand and waiting to be called upon in class, especially when an instructor stood before the class and asked an open question. The boy didn't realize that the question was not directed to him personally but was being asked of the entire class with the expectation that hands would be raised in response. He instead blurted out his responses in ways that were considered socially inept. As you can imagine, this was stigmatizing for him, and his misunderstanding of the situation was interpreted as being deliberately disruptive, which was not the case. Gray resolved this by providing the boy with a brief, bullet-point sequence of sentences that created a story to convey the proper protocol for raising one's hand. (For further information about Gray's specific Social Story formula, refer to her books listed in Appendix A.)

The concept is not unlike the crib notes or "cheat sheets" that you may have used in school to jog your memory in retaining pertinent information. It's the same thing here, and once the boy memorized the story, he was able to automatically remember the proper thing to do and say. Stories such as these are a tangible, concrete way of demystifying the particulars of social situations or environments that may cause apprehension, anxiety, or distress. This strategy has been tremendously successful with children with Asperger's and autism. When you create these stories, it is important to keep in mind the following:

- Keep the stories simple, with a clear beginning and end.

- Follow a clear-cut, logical sequence.

- Try to keep the story to one page in length.

- Don't state anything definitively without allowance for mistakes (we're all human, after all). For example, "I will try to remember to ask to use the CD player." Instead of "I will always remember . . . ."

- Allow the story to become your child's personal property to review at her leisure.

- Review it with her regularly outside of the situation that the story was written to explain.

- Fade out (meaning use less frequently) or discard the story once it's no longer needed.

- The story may be portable, but keep it discreetly in a pocket or inside a notebook (or day planner).

Your child may personalize the story and take a greater interest in "owning" it if she is given the opportunity to illustrate it.

Spirituality

As a person who may be naturally, inherently gentle and sensitive, your child also may possess an innate sense of spirituality. This doesn't necessarily refer to being religious, but rather spiritual in having a deep appreciation for the beauty in everything and everyone around him. These are the children who are drawn to the tiny details in nature.

> You may find that spirituality is integral in your approach to conscious parenting. Prayer, meditation, or simply quiet reflection will reduce stress and re-energize you as well as provide you with clarity. Being aware of your full, deliberate breaths, even if only for a moment or two, will create an overall sensation of peacefulness.

Your child's heightened sensitivity may also predispose her to being finely attuned to her environment. She may sense things that others do not—or cannot—readily perceive. If you see this in your child, you've likely seen it from a very early age. Your child may have had powerful dreams, intuitions, or premonitions that proved accurate, or other experiences of a spiritual nature that some would call uncanny coincidences. There are simply some aspects of the human experience that traditional science cannot measure and quantify, such as love or faith.

It is important to assume several responsibilities if your child has such heightened sensitivities:

O Accept it as a natural extension of who she is.

O Do not arbitrarily dismiss it or make your child feel in any way unfit or afraid to discuss her sensitivities.

○ Do not sensationalize it by exaggerating it, blowing it out of proportion, or openly sharing it with others without your child's knowledge (remember disclosure?).

○ Keep it confidential except to reveal information to those who can be trusted to understand unconditionally.

○ Remember that intermittent experiences do not a mental illness make. Review the mental health chapter again if you have concerns; common mental health diagnoses are determined by groupings of symptoms, not by sporadic, unexplainable instances.

○ Accept what your child tells you to be the truth as she knows it.

As your child enters adolescence and adulthood, her sense of spirituality and commitment of faith to a higher authority may be the very thing that pulls her through rough times. Having these values instilled in her early on in life could prove to be her single most important resource.

Important Points to Consider

Most parents want to teach their children the skills to help them gain independence, but this is especially important if your child has Asperger's Syndrome. Your child must understand herself and her condition well enough that she can tell when things are going downhill and know how to ask for help for herself. Here are some important points to keep in mind:

○ Help your child create a schedule so she can see what her days ahead will bring. Children with Asperger's often like to be in the know and not have any surprises, and a detailed schedule of events will let her focus and feel prepared.

○ Partner with your child to find a touchstone that she can use when she feels that things are getting out of control. The touchstone is a comfort object that can be touched or stroked in difficult times to bring about a sense of calm. Help your child find an object that means something to her and will bring her comfort when she needs it most.

○ Teach your child a "social out." Give her a way to excuse herself from difficult situations that will not be perceived as socially odd. In this way your child can leave a situation that is causing anxiety before a meltdown occurs.

○ Respect your child's social out. If you hear your child use her social out, do not force her to wait or tell her to tough it out. Build trust with your child by honoring her call for help.

Transitioning to Adulthood

The greatest challenge you will face as a parent of a child with Asperger's Syndrome is supporting him through the transition to adulthood. As protective as you may be with all your children, at some point you will be ready for your child with Asperger's to leave home and venture out on his own into the adult world. Of course your relationship is not severed, and your loving support can ease your child into the often-intimidating arena of adult responsibilities.

Planning for the Future

In addition to your child's transitional Individualized Education Program, you may wish to consider initiating person-centered planning meetings as your child prepares to graduate high school. If your school district is open to it, and if stipulated in the IEP, the person-centered planning process can dovetail nicely with a transition plan, or the two can be folded together. In fact, the person-centered plan may be more comprehensive in terms of a vision for your child's future.

In the person-centered planning process, the individual remains the focus, but meeting participants include family, friends, relatives, and any others who know the individual well and with whom the individual has a personal history. There are a wide variety of person-centered plan formats that may be referred to by different names, such as self-determination, personal futures planning, person-centered development, or lifestyle blueprint. The components of each are essentially the same; they are just packaged a bit differently.

The focus of person-centered planning is on identifying the individual's talents, gifts, and skills. The focus is *not* to identify all of the individual's perceived "deficiencies" with the goal of plugging those needs into traditional or stereotyped opportunities in order to build skills the team believes are lacking. Common aspects of person-centered planning include:

- The person as the primary focus

- Involvement of participants who know the person and care about him

- Exploring individual capacity, hopes, reservations, dreams, and preferences

- Helping the person to attain a desirable future

- Ensuring the safety and well-being of the person's emotional, mental, and physical health

- Creating systems changes wherever possible with creative thinking and innovative strategies—thinking outside the box

Cornell University's Employment and Disability Institute offers a wide variety of person-centered planning information on their website, *www.personcenteredplanning.org*. These resources include online self-study courses and person-centered planning tools that may be used as guides or templates when gathering to discuss an individual's future pathways. Additional links and downloadable information may also be found on this website.

It is a plan created by a network of people who are committed to supporting an individual to envision a desirable future, but it is that person's vision and not what others wish for him. While the planning process is one that evolves and changes as it continues over time (this means more than one meeting is involved), it is a process that is outcome-based. The intended outcomes include:

○ The person will have an enhanced life.

○ Relationships or friendships will grow.

○ The person will contribute in ways that are meaningful or functional.

○ Expression of individual choices, wants, dreams, and desires is valued.

○ The person will feel more a part of the community.

The Person-Centered Planning Process

In order to plan for a smooth person-centered planning process, in partnership with your child first identify those individuals he'd like present. Perhaps he'd like to send out invitations and make menu selections for refreshments as well. The meeting will benefit from having a facilitator who is neutral (perhaps unrelated to the situation entirely) and who can:

- Keep the focus on your child

- Manage and be remindful of time

- Record and disperse meeting minutes

- Follow up with participants, including keeping track of the status of commitments and scheduling future meetings

The facilitator will gently guide the meeting, not control it. Ideally, this person will also help your child and his team visually map the flow of the discussion on an overhead projector, flip chart, blackboard, or large pieces of paper tacked to the wall. The simplest format of a person-centered plan might ask your child and his team questions about what he wishes to accomplish in areas of education and training, employment, recreation, and community living. The focus should be positive and proactive; worry about deconstructing obstacles later. When this doesn't occur, the meeting can quickly digress into a lot of statements like, "We can't do that because . . . ."

The facilitator should also ensure that everyone uses respectful language; this is definitely not a time to rehash unflattering incidents that will cause your child public embarrassment. If concerns arise, remind all participants that any discussion must occur with your child's personal and informed choice. The mutual understanding should be that personal and informed choice covers the areas of health, safety, and personal welfare.

When preparing for a person-centered plan meeting, be sure to hold it in an environment that's as comfortable and informal as possible in a neutral setting (somewhere other than a professional office or conference room). Snacks and refreshments are always helpful to increase the comfort level of all participants, especially if formal relationships have previously been strained. Remember, in this meeting no one has any authority to make anyone do anything; it's about agreements, promises, and commitments.

The duration of the meeting depends upon the stamina of the team, but it is advisable not to go longer than a couple of hours. Remember, a person-centered plan is a dynamic process that plays out over time. There will be future opportunities to continue dialogues begun at the first meeting. Depending upon the areas identified for each section of the person-centered plan format (regardless of which format is used), there will be assignments made for roles, responsibilities, and time frames for implementation of the plan. Participants, including you and your child, should commit to their responsibilities, be in contact with other team members between meetings (mass e-mailings accomplish this well), and be able to update the team on progress made at each meeting.

Barriers to the person-centered plan process may include:

○ Uncertainty about what your child wants (perhaps he hasn't learned to dream or is afraid to)

○ Breakdowns or stalemates in communication

○ Family expectations versus your child's dreams and wishes

○ Conflicting values among team members

○ Funding and other system limitations

○ Time commitment and responsibilities being too labor-intensive for some team members to be effective

Remember that a person-centered plan is an actual document, a tool that becomes your child's property. It should be revisited and revised as often as necessary. Those involved in the process need to honor their commitments and be willing to "shift gears" as needs arise to alter the plan's course.

The outcome of the initial person-centered plan meeting should be a document that details how best to support your child's future. If you can gather together a strong, supportive team of people committed to helping your child transition to adulthood, a person-centered plan can be a useful tool in devising a visual blueprint for moving forward.

Independent Living

Moving out of your home will be a major life step for your child. Assisting him in finding a living place in the community may depend upon several things:

O Affordable, acceptable housing

O Geographic proximity to you and areas of the community accessed by your child

O Your child's ability to support himself

O Funds you are able and willing to contribute to supporting your child

O Outside resources for funding or housing

Regrettably, there are far more resources available for community living for people with mental retardation or mental health issues than for folks with Asperger's Syndrome. The person with Asperger's may present as able-bodied, intelligent, and perfectly capable of caring for himself. When families wish to access services and supports, it may prompt accusations from others that they are attempting to unnecessarily "play" the system, because the subtleties of Asperger's make the need for services less apparent. As you well know, however, the needs are real, and identifying and selecting a living arrangement away from your home can be a time of apprehension and uncertainty for all.

Learning New Responsibilities

Issues that may arise during the transition to independent living will likely be followed by lots of anxiety for you and, especially, for your child. If your child has had no previous experience with balancing a budget, maintaining a checkbook, paying bills, grocery shopping, and interacting with a landlord, you both could be in for a rude awakening as your child acclimates himself to life away from home. If your child is renting an apartment, ensure that he has a clear understanding of the landlord's rules and expectations. If this understanding is not clear from the landlord's contract, support your child to extract the key components and create a separate, written document for handy reference.

In one instance, a young man with Asperger's came home to his apartment to find a note from the landlord informing him that new carpet was going to be installed on a certain date and that the young man would have to move many of his personal possessions. Never before having been in such a situation, the young man believed that paying for the carpet was his responsibility. He panicked, realizing that he didn't have enough money to cover such an expense (and knowing no ally was immediately available to him). He was also upset that his things had to be moved.

Partner with your child to set up his living space in a way that is comfortable for him, complies with any formal terms of agreement (such as a lease), and meets your satisfaction about safety issues. Consider the following adaptations to your child's independent living space:

- Ensure that all smoke detectors are functional and that your child knows the fire escape route (stress that this is a precaution for everyone; otherwise, you may incite undue anxiety about the likelihood of a fire).

- Purchase a fire extinguisher and practice using it.

- Get a phone with automatic dial or push-button photos of familiar people whose numbers are called often or who should be called in an emergency (especially if your child becomes easily flustered or forgetful when upset).

- Purchase a monthly bill organizer with slots that correspond to specific dates to indicate what gets paid when to help your child stay focused and up-to-date when keeping track of bills. Or, set your child up to pay bills electronically online.

- Get a large wall calendar with large blocks for each day on which to make notes as a useful visual.

○ If your child is not well organized or is forgetful, ask him to post a simple checklist by the door (listing things such as checking to make sure lights are off, no faucets are running, appliances are turned off, etc.) to run through each time he leaves home.

You will wish to add to this list as the need arises, but ensure that you are not being overbearing and overly protective. Living independently may well be a step that your child has wanted to take for some time. Enter into this step of the journey in partnership, and listen to what your child is saying he wants.

Many mail order companies offer diverse and eclectic novelty-type devices that may be of good use to the child transitioning to his or her own living space in the community. One such business, Sky Mall (*www.skymall.com* or 1-800-SKYMALL), offers many state-of-the-art items designed for adaptability and security purposes, including monthly bill organizers and other organizing devices, photo-button phones, soothing alarm clocks, and sound-muffling appliances.

Don't Get Taken Advantage Of

Unless you've taught your child to crack the code of social slang and innuendo as it applies to various circumstances, he may take what others say at face value and do what they ask of him without question. He may do this because he's a pleaser and wants to be accepted, especially in his new community residence or apartment. However, unless he knows to report an unethical situation, your child may become an easy mark for others to deliberately abuse and take advantage of. Once again, this is where having a close ally, or allies, is significant in the life of your child. Case managers and social workers are required to touch base with individuals on their caseload, but often that happens infrequently, especially for people under their supervision who are considered "high functioning" and largely independent. Your child needs someone he can contact daily if needed.

Some of the ways your child may be taken advantage of include:

○ Others extorting money from him, even under the guise of giving to a charity or worthy cause

○ Being deceived into doing something illegal, such as delivering drugs to another individual

○ Being verbally, physically, or sexually abused, or deceived into doing these things to others

○ Being pressured or deceived into giving away, or selling at a nominal fee, personal possessions, appliances, jewelry, etc.

○ Being made to feel accepted by becoming an accomplice to a crime, such as shoplifting

○ Succumbing to every telemarketer, or otherwise freely giving out confidential information such as a Social Security number or loaning credit cards or an ATM card to others

○ Giving out copies of one's residence key or allowing others to freely use his home and personal property

○ Regularly loaning his car to others

In raising your child, you have done your parental best to teach him right from wrong. Now more than ever you will want to ensure that your child is clear that anything that doesn't look, sound, or feel "right" or seems too good to be true is cause for extreme caution. Manipulative people can be masterful in deceiving others who are perceived as naive and gullible. One young man ran up huge credit card bills because he felt compelled to buy a lot of the merchandise advertised on TV in "act now, supplies limited" offers. He needed extra assistance in budgeting his money and recognizing his financial limitations.

This information is not to dissuade you from pursuing independent living for your child; rather, it is merely to serve as a caution as you and your child move forward.

Understanding Justice

Children with Asperger's can have a very rigid sense of justice and injustice. That is, black is black and white is white with no gray in between. The gray, of course, does exist in life, but learning this may well be a confusing process for your child. This is why driving a car can be problematic for some people; careful adherence to the rules of the road doesn't mean that everyone else is following the same rules as correctly as you are. In fact, when driving, everyone regularly "fudges" and, technically speaking, breaks minor rules or laws all the time to suit his or her personal convenience, such as exceeding the speed limit or not coming to a complete stop at stop signs.

EXPLAINING THE CONCEPT OF JUSTICE

Communicating the concept of justice versus injustice to your child can be difficult, especially in relation to his own behavior and actions. Wherever possible, use anecdotes from your child's past without sounding punitive or accusatory. Though your child may become highly defensive of his motives for doing something, remind him that, as a parent, you made the judgment that he was in error, if that is the case. There may also have been times when a sibling, neighbor, or cousin reported to you that your child did something that you considered minor enough not to act upon. You may wish to reveal those instances to your child as well. Revisiting this topic over time, or as the need arises, will be a "safe" way for your child to practice developing the skill to make judgment calls about those gray areas.

It can be just as difficult for your child to determine when the actions of another are cause for concern. One way to help your child understand this is to discuss it in the context of whether or not the act is harmful to others. Some people with Asperger's who live in the community become nuisances because they repeatedly dial 911 to report a wide variety of infractions that they perceive as legitimate but that are not appropriate to report as emergencies. Coach your child on weighing the potential ramifications of reporting something that either doesn't directly affect him or doesn't cause harm to others or their property. You may even wish to create a visual guessing game using words, pictures, or YouTube videos and pausing to brainstorm with your child about each specific scenario. Are there real-life scenarios either of you can recall that mirror your discussion (and reinforce the concept in a concrete manner)? If you use the TV shows or characters that most impassion your child, this learning time will be especially pleasing and memorable.

THE ROLE OF THE POLICE

Police academies across the country are slowly becoming more aware of the responsibility law enforcement officials have to broaden their knowledge about people with different ways of being. California and Pennsylvania are among the leaders in this initiative. You may wish to contact your local police headquarters or state police academy to learn about the status of police training on people with special needs. If you are affiliated with any autism or Asperger's groups in your area, you may wish to volunteer your time and services to support your local police in this endeavor.

WHAT TO DO WHEN STOPPED

If stopped and questioned by a police officer, your child can protect himself by quietly listening to and complying with the officer's directions, such as a request to put down what's in one's hand (if a weapon is suspected). As always, disclosing one's diagnosis in the moment is a personal choice, and stating, "I have Asperger's Syndrome" may or may not have relevance for a police officer at the time. Anyone can become quickly flustered or rattled if stopped by a police officer. You may forget information that you should be able to readily provide, or you may feel justified in blurting out your side of the story. If your child chooses not to disclose his diagnosis, as is his right, he may have to communicate his confusion in order to understand and cooperate with the police officer. An example may be to say, "You're talking too fast, please slow down." Or "I don't understand what you're asking, please say it another way." Your child may also want to ask that the officer call you or an ally to be present with you.

Misunderstandings

Because people with Asperger's can be pleasers, or perhaps very frightened in the moment, some folks have confessed to crimes they didn't commit in order to end the interrogation or satisfy the inquiring officer. In one instance, a twenty-year-old man with Asperger's entered into a sexual relationship with a neighbor. Later, when the relationship soured, the woman formally accused the young man of sexual assault. Because of his diagnosis, his confusion about details, and his misunderstanding of the legal system, his side of the story was not believed and he found himself incarcerated, serving a sentence for what his family believes was an entirely consensual relationship.

A STALKING CHARGE

If your child is involved in a romantic relationship that is not being reciprocated, monitor the situation as cautiously as you can to guard against your child's actions and activities being construed as stalking. When some individuals with Asperger's fall in love, it can appear to be an obsession or infatuation. While the individual's feelings are genuine and sincere, his or her expression of those feelings, through words and actions, can seem exaggerated. The desire to express love can come across as desperate and even urgent, the intensity of which may be quite frightening to the person on the receiving end—especially if he or she no longer wishes to participate in the relationship.

Stalking is defined differently by each state. The National Center for Victims of Crime is a clearinghouse for stalking-related information. The Center's website is *www.victimsofcrime.org*. It provides state-by-state and federal statutes, help for victims, stalking profiles, statistics, and other resources.

HARASSMENT OR ASSAULT

Your child may be genuinely surprised to learn that something he has done is criminal or constitutes unacceptable behavior. Sometimes this occurs because of how films and TV portray relationships between people. So much of what is considered to be entertainment is over-the-top, exaggerated human behavior. Most people would never dream of engaging in some of the activities they see or saying the things movie characters say, because they know they'd get arrested, fired from their jobs, or damage relationships. Part of the entertainment comes from the comfort and safety of watching what happens to someone who so blatantly breaks the social code of acceptable conduct.

So, for example, in a movie, the leading man can say to a woman, "Hey babe, nice rack! Let's go get it on!" and it works. If your child used this line in real life, he would probably be slapped across the face (in the best-case scenario) or have sexual harassment charges filed against him (in the worst-case scenario). Many instances of alleged sexual harassment by young men with Asperger's are later determined to be misinterpretations along these lines.

Calling the Police

If your child is living independently in the community, it will be important to discuss emergency situations and when it is advisable to call 911 or the local police. Your child has certain sensitivities and ways of doing things that may not mesh well with what others consider "typical." This has the potential to create conflict for your child. Your child may find himself in altercations with neighbors, other tenants, or people in the community.

If your child is without an ally to help sort things through, he may be prone to blowing situations out of proportion. Your child may exaggerate things that other, less-sensitive people may consider simply ignorant or mildly offensive. When this happens, your child may believe he is justified in calling the police. It is important to help your child understand what types of situations warrant police intervention, as well as the priority level of those that do.

When a police call comes in, time and effort are required to ascertain its priority. Calls such as loud music complaints may well be considered "low priority," depending upon call volume and the flexibility of the police force on duty. That a call is low priority may or may not be communicated to the caller. It can be problematic for the person with Asperger's, whose acute hearing is deafened by a neighbor's music, to be told "it will be a while" or "an officer will be out in about an hour" when calling to complain. This vague response may cause the person to repeatedly call back to follow up, thus increasing everyone's frustration and anxiety.

Remember, police have authority over crime and criminal behavior, not civil issues. It may be a shock for your child (and perhaps you) to learn that there are certain civil issues over which police have limited influence or control, or are considered "iffy" in terms of interpretation. These may include:

O Most circumstances involving landlords—a huge issue for lots of adults with Asperger's who feel mistreated or ignored

O Verbal agreements with others, such as loaning someone a cell phone and not getting it back, or not getting it back by an agreed-upon date

O Children under ten (who cannot be arrested) running in and out of a yard, or whose ball, for example, keeps bouncing into your yard

O Certain types of speech, such as someone saying mean things

Unless there's reason to believe there is criminal intent against your child, such as plotting harm, these areas are largely beyond police purview. If there are valid concerns that are police responsibility but are also considered low priority, it will behoove your child to track the concerns through written documentation that includes dates, times, and succinct descriptions of the offending activity. Acts of criminal mischief, trespassing, or disturbance of the peace, like dogs barking or loud music, are offenses for which the perpetrator may receive a warning or a citation. Depending upon the severity of the situation, it may be that your child can attempt to resolve the situation in a neighborly and civil manner.

Important Points to Consider

Planning for the future of your child with Asperger's Syndrome may seem daunting, but as in most things related to Asperger's, preparation is the key to preventing problems. Many of the stages of growing independence, such as moving out on his own, may be riddled with anxiety-causing issues, and it is important that you coach your child through what should happen and what concerns he should keep an eye out for. Here are some points to keep in mind:

○ Children with Asperger's are generally pleasers, and this means they may trust too easily, and trust the wrong people. Be sure to communicate with your child about what is acceptable behavior and when others may be taking advantage of him.

○ Prepare your child for independent life by helping him organize and prepare for his daily tasks of living, such as paying rent or other bills.

○ Talk honestly with your child about dating interactions and how to read other people's signals and cues. Often people with Asperger's misunderstand the advances of others, which can lead to issues like stalking or obsessive behavior.

○ Many children with Asperger's view any small infraction of justice as a tremendous crime that must be reported to the police. Communicate with your child about what makes a real issue for the police and which things may not be included in the policeman's role.

 **CHAPTER 16**

The Rewards of Being an Asperger's Parent

If you have used your mindful practices to see the glass half full instead of half empty, then you have recognized the profound journey upon which you've embarked as a parent. Parents of children with different ways of being can lead lives that are often complex and complicated by their child's difference. Often such complications are imposed by others who do not understand or appreciate your child's way of being in the world. But, the two most important things you can do for your child with Asperger's are to value, encourage, and indulge his most passionate interests (with an eye toward a future vocation) and to foster the development of a relationship with at least one ally. In so doing, your child will be better poised to prosper in life.

What Have You Learned?

Think back to the moment you first received your child's diagnosis of Asperger's Syndrome or ASD. What were you feeling in that moment? Confusion? Upset? Despair? Hopelessness? Next, think about how you're feeling now, today, especially after having read this book. How much different do you feel now compared with then?

You and your child have been on quite a journey together. She has worked to adapt to people, places, and things that are often very difficult to discern without your gentle support and guidance. Your child has come a long way toward becoming more self-sufficient and independent. But what about you? What have you learned as an Asperger's parent? One mom, Gina, eloquently summarizes her thoughts and feelings in a way that many parents will relate to best.

> I've always thought of having a child with Asperger's Syndrome as a journey. It begins with the never-to-be-forgotten moment the words tumble out of a physician's mouth. Little do any of us realize it at the time, but the whole world is about to change forever. Sometimes there is grief, sometimes despair. Yet there are also times of such profound revelation, such profound love, that you find yourself thanking God that he gave you this incredible being who inevitably expanded you and taught you so much.
>
> In the early days, I remember thinking, "Why me? Why Jon?" One day the answer came to me. "Why not me? Why not my son?" If there was to be a child with Asperger's, perhaps I was the perfect person to be that child's parent. And perhaps I needed that child just as much as he needed me. I am forever changed because of it. And I cannot imagine being anyone but the person I am today. If Jon is a special-needs kid, then maybe I'm a special-needs parent.

Another equally wise mother shared her observations as well:

> Your job, like Edison's mother, is to develop the child's potential, which may be greater (or not) than your own. You are helping him to unlock his world. You deepen your relationship with the child. He may share some insights only with you, about himself or about what he is learning or creating. What a privilege!

Bonnie, another mother, believes in using her son Noel's passions to gain access to his way of thinking. Not only has this made the teaching and learning process easier and more effective, but she has had the pleasure of seeing her son learn and achieve. In so doing, Bonnie has found that she's learned a lot about herself, and she calls the special bond with Noel "an amazing experience."

As a parent who practices mindfulness, you have harvested a substantial reserve of pleasing memories about raising your child with Asperger's Syndrome. Never underestimate the potential you have to influence other parents who may be feeling overwhelmed. A kind word of optimism will create a ripple effect when that person feels empowered to pay it forward.

Without your child in your life, you would be a different person, wouldn't you? As the parent of a child with Asperger's Syndrome, how has your life been "forever changed"? Perhaps you have become stronger, more vocal, or more defensive in protection of your child and her rights. (By extension, are you more tolerant and compassionate of differences in people of all kinds?) Perhaps your example of total, loving acceptance has been the model others follow, including your other children. Remember that your children will reflect back to you what you project upon them. Armed with your loving support, your trust, and your confidence, your child with Asperger's will be poised for great things. And you have every reason to expect them.

As a simple exercise, develop a written list of all the things you've learned from your child with Asperger's Syndrome. The list may include items that are academic in nature, inspired by her most passionate of interests, or lessons about sensitivity toward others, or patience. It may be a powerful thing to lovingly share your list with your child, perhaps at a special event like a sixteenth or twenty-first birthday or a graduation.

Asperger's and the World

As society learns more about autism and Asperger's Syndrome, a burgeoning community of support has developed. Parents are no longer content to accept the often very limiting parameters of the current federal, state, and local service systems available to children with differences. Instead they are becoming impassioned advocates, creating inroads, shaping laws, and dictating what is and what is not acceptable for their children. As you've learned, parents have long-established formal and informal local networks, accessible through state and county social service systems. A resource list, included at the back of this book as Appendix B, highlights some of the many online Asperger's Syndrome groups organized to educate, enlighten, and entertain individuals, families, friends, and the community.

In seeking formal and informal supports for your child, don't be surprised if you are both a recipient of service and an educator to others. Many traditional services are based on a medical or mental retardation model, and not an autism or Asperger's service delivery model. As always, encourage your child to be her own best advocate.

Your child, teenager, or young adult with Asperger's may feel isolated and estranged from others who share her similarities. Forging friendships with like others is a personal choice that may be of little to no consequence to your child, especially if she is comfortable with the number of healthy relationships in her life. Still others seek a kinship that may not be readily found in one's hometown. Computer technology and the Internet have revolutionized the world, and, in particular, have been a blessing for the person with Asperger's Syndrome for reasons previously outlined. It is entirely possible for your child to communicate with others around the world who are also seeking a connectedness in learning about Asperger's Syndrome and themselves. From the comfort of her home, your child can converse with others; understand more about herself; feel joy and relief in comparing daily challenges others face; and vent about the general intolerance of the "big world." Through these relationships, your child may develop an enhanced confidence and comfort level about Asperger's—it's really not so different after all. Opportunities to meet in person, to make formal presentations, or to contribute to various online and hard-copy publications may be available. It is a rare individual with Asperger's who does not desire to educate others.

The Neurodiversity Movement

As individuals with Asperger's Syndrome are coming into their own, many are finding solace, camaraderie, and political awareness through local meeting groups, national conferences, and Internet communities online. Many such individuals decry the common mindset that autism and Asperger's should be perceived as every bit as curable as a disease; instead, growing numbers have banded together in a human rights movement to promote acceptance for their different way of being. It even has a name: neurodiversity, that is, the full inclusion and equality of people who think, learn, process, and interact differently than the average or "neurotypical" person. Online websites include *www.wrongplanet.net*, *www.grasp.org*, and *www.aspiesforfreedom.com*, which suggests a concept that is new to many—"Asperger's and autism are not negative, and are not always a disability." (These Internet groups welcome the support, participation, and questions of parents and caregivers.)

Your child with Asperger's may well find it comforting to discover allies—or even a political calling—by accessing one or more of these groups. Such was the case for Ari Ne'eman, a young man with Asperger's who has, in short order, risen to national prominence and political appointment for his work as a self-advocate.

Other well-known self-advocates with Asperger's who have established national reputations as authors, consultants, and presenters include Michael John Carley, Dr. Nick Dubin, Brian King, Jerry Newport, Dr. Stephen Shore, and John Elder Robison. One day soon, your child may join this roster of those fostering social change and cultural competency if she so chooses.

The Future

Ultimately, we are all temporary in the lives of the people we know and love. After you have passed on, your wish for your child may include that she be surrounded with a circle of loved ones and friends, to be successfully employed, and to be well accepted—if not revered—in her chosen community. Hopefully, this introduction to Asperger's Syndrome has provided you with philosophies and strategies that match well with your role as a parent. Use what makes sense and leave behind what does not. You may wish to use this book as a springboard to others that are more specific and technical, or you may wish to read about people who have encountered, lived with, or loved someone with Asperger's Syndrome.

Contemplating your child's future may feel discouraging. As a mindful parent, don't sweat the small stuff; focus on it instead! Pay attention to the details of your interactions with your child in the moment. Not only will you enjoy the enhancement to your relationship, but your attunement to details is in keeping with how your child with Asperger's sees the world.

As we look to the future, we are seeing a growing acceptance in our culture of all people with different ways of being. The language we use to describe people's differences is no longer a matter of "political correctness"—it is a show of renewed respect. In this day and age, no one can justly define "normal" or "typical." Not one of us can say we don't know someone with a difference or disability. This may include the woman who's had a mastectomy, the man who developed Parkinson's disease, the teenager with an eating disorder, or the child with Down Syndrome. At some point, we will collectively recognize that all ways of being, including Asperger's Syndrome, are simply a normal part of being human. After all, we're all more alike than different.

Appendix A:
Further Reading

Aston, Maxine. *Aspergers in Love: Couple Relationships and Family Affairs* (London: Jessica Kingsley Publishers, Ltd., 2003).

Attwood, Tony. *Asperger's Syndrome: A Guide for Parents and Professionals* (London: Jessica Kingsley Publishers, Ltd., 1998).

Birch, Jen. *Congratulations! It's Asperger Syndrome* (London: Jessica Kingsley Publishers, Ltd., 2003).

Boyd, Brenda. *Parenting a Child with Asperger Syndrome: 200 Tips and Strategies* (London: Jessica Kingsley Publishers, Ltd., 2003).

Carley, Michael John. *Asperger's from the Inside Out: A Supportive and Practical Guide for Anyone with Asperger's Syndrome* (New York: Perigee Trade, 2008).

Cohen, Shirley. *Targeting Autism: What We Know, Don't Know, and Can Do to Help Young Children with Autism Spectrum Disorders, 3rd Edition* (Berkeley: University of California Press, 2006).

Cook O'Toole, Jennifer. *The Asperkid's Secret Book of Social Rules: The Handbook of Not-So-Obvious Social Guidelines for Tweens & Teens with Asperger Syndrome* (London: Jessica Kingsley Publishers, Ltd., 2014).

Delaney, Tara. *101 Games and Activities for Children with Autism, Asperger's, and Sensory Processing Disorders* (McGraw-Hill Education, 2009).

Dubin, Nick. *Asperger Syndrome and Anxiety: A Guide to Successful Stress Management* (London: Jessica Kingsley Publishers, Ltd., 2009).

Faherty, Catherine. *Autism . . . What Does It Mean to Me?: A Workbook about Self-Awareness and Life Lessons for Kids with Autism or Asperger's* (Arlington, TX: Future Horizons, Inc., 2014).

Grandin, Temple. *Thinking in Pictures and Other Reports from My Life with Autism* (New York: Doubleday, 1995).

Gray, Carol. *The New Social Story Book: Illustrated Edition* (Arlington, TX: Future Horizons, Inc., 2000).

Grossberg, Blythe. *Asperger's Rules! How to Make Sense of School and Friends* (Magination Press, 2012).

Holliday Willey, Liane. *Pretending to Be Normal: Living with Asperger's Syndrome, Expanded Edition* (London: Jessica Kingsley Publishers, Ltd., 2014).

____. *Asperger Syndrome in the Family: Redefining Normal* (London: Jessica Kingsley Publishers, Ltd., 2001).

Jackson, Luke. *Freaks, Geeks & Asperger Syndrome: A User Guide to Adolescence* (London: Jessica Kingsley Publishers, Ltd., 2002).

Kephart, Beth. *A Slant of Sun: One Child's Courage* (New York: W.W. Norton & Company, Inc., 1998).

Lawson, Wendy. *Build Your Own Life: A Self-Help Guide for Individuals with Asperger's Syndrome* (London: Jessica Kingsley Publishers, Ltd., 2003).

Meyer, Roger N. *Asperger Syndrome Employment Workbook: An Employment Workbook for Adults with Asperger Syndrome* (London: Jessica Kingsley Publishers, Ltd., 2001).

Moyes, Rebecca A. *Incorporating Social Goals in the Classroom: A Guide for Teachers and Parents of Children with High-Functioning Autism and Asperger Syndrome* (London: Jessica Kingsley Publishers, Ltd., 2001).

____. *Addressing the Challenging Behavior of Children with High-Functioning Autism/Asperger Syndrome in the Classroom: A Guide for Teachers and Parents* (London: Jessica Kingsley Publishers, Ltd., 2002).

Nash, J. Madeleine. "The Secrets of Autism," *Time*, 6 May 2002.

O'Neill, Jasmine Lee. *Through the Eyes of Aliens: A Book About Autistic People* (London: Jessica Kingsley Publishers, Ltd., 1999).

Papolos, Demitri, and Janice Papolos. *The Bipolar Child: The Definitive and Reassuring Guide to Childhood's Most Misunderstood Disorder, 3rd Edition* (New York: Broadway Books, 2006).

Pyles, Lise. *Hitchhiking through Asperger Syndrome* (London: Jessica Kingsley Publishers, Ltd., 2002).

Robison, John Elder. *Look Me in the Eye: My Life with Asperger's* (New York: Crown, 2007).

Simone, Rudy. *Aspergirls: Empowering Females with Asperger Syndrome* (London: Jessica Kingsley Publishers, Ltd., 2010).

Stanford, Ashley. *Asperger Syndrome and Long-Term Relationships* (London: Jessica Kingsley Publishers, Ltd., 2003).

Stillman, William. *Demystifying the Autistic Experience: A Humanistic Introduction for Parents, Caregivers and Educators* (London: Jessica Kingsley Publishers, Ltd., 2002).

_____. *Empowered Autism Parenting: Celebrating (and Defending) Your Child's Place in the World* (San Francisco: Jossey-Bass, 2009).

Winter, Matt. *Asperger Syndrome: What Teachers Need to Know, 2nd Edition* (London: Jessica Kingsley Publishers, Ltd., 2011).

Wylie, Philip. *Very Late Diagnosis of Asperger Syndrome (Autism Spectrum Disorder): How Seeking a Diagnosis in Adulthood Can Change Your Life* (London: Jessica Kingsley Publishers, Ltd., 2014).

Appendix B:
Website Resources

www.aane.org
Asperger/Autism Network fosters awareness, respect, acceptance, and support for people with Asperger's and their families.

www.autismnetworkinternational.org
Autism Network International. A self-help and advocacy organization run by people with autism for people on the autism spectrum.

www.aspennj.org
ASPEN (Autism Spectrum Education Network), headquartered in New Jersey.

www.aspergersyndrome.org
Online Asperger Syndrome Information and Support (OASIS) and MAAP Services for Autism and Asperger Syndrome, a site originally created by parents.

www.aspie.com
Website of Liane Holliday Willey, Asperger's Syndrome self-advocate and author.

www.asplint.com
ASPies LInking with NeuroTypicals (ASPLINT), website of Dr. Jeffrey Deutsch, life coach and person with Asperger's, which includes employment information.

www.autismasperger.net
Website of Stephen Shore, Asperger's Syndrome self-advocate, consultant, and author.

www.autismservicescenter.org
The Autism Services Center, a national autism hotline and website.

www.autismspeaks.org
Website of the United States' largest autism organization. Request the Asperger's Tool Kit for comprehensive tips, strategies, and information.

www.autism-society.org
Autism Society of America.

www.danmarinofoundation.org
The Dan Marino Foundation.

www.disabilityisnatural.com
Website of Kathie Snow, disability rights activist and parent.

www.donnawilliams.net
A prominent autism self-advocate and author.

www.flutiefoundation.org
The Doug Flutie Jr. Foundation for Autism, Inc.

www.ed.gov
U.S. Department of Education.

www.feat.org
Families for Early Autism Treatment.

www.grasp.org
The Global and Regional Asperger Syndrome Partnership (GRASP). An informational, educational, and advocacy organization operated by people on the autism spectrum.

www.thegraycenter.org
Website of special educator and social stories founder Carol Gray.

www.lookingupautism.org
Monthly international autism newsletter.

www.nacdd.org
National Association of Councils on Developmental Disabilities.

www.neurodiversity.com
An extensive collection of information "honoring the variety of human wiring" that also includes national news reports on the abuses committed against people with autism.

www.ninds.nih.gov/disorders/autism/autism.htm
National Institutes of Health autism website.

www.ont-autism.uoguelph.ca
Ontario Adult Autism Research and Support Network (OAARSN).

www.P2PUSA.org
National Parent to Parent Network.

https://www.autismspeaks.org/family-services/autism-safety-project/first-responders/law-enforcement
An Autism Speaks web page for facts and resources about autism and law enforcement.

www.templegrandin.com
Temple Grandin. Perhaps the best-known autism self-advocate and bestselling author.

www.wrightslaw.org
The website of Peter Wright, Esquire, an expert on special education.

Index